…EAL GHOSTBUSTER

MEMOIRS OF AN EXORCIST

This edition first published in Great Britain in 2006 by Sevenoaks
20 Mortimer Street
London W1T 3JW

10-digit ISBN 1-86200-340-8
13-digit ISBN 978-1-86200-340-8

Typeset by E-Type, Liverpool
Printed and bound in Great Britain by Mackays

THE REAL GHOSTBUSTER

MEMOIRS OF AN EXORCIST

DAVID DEVEREUX

SevenOaks

THANKS

There are a number of people without whom this book would not have come to pass, and I think it's only fair that I thank them publicly so you all know who to blame:

My colleagues at Athanor, those not named herein as well as those which are, because this has been one hell of a ride so far. It's one I intend to continue, and I'm proud to have them all as friends as well as comrades in arms.

Steve Jackson, who suggested writing this book in the first place. It is, therefore, all his fault.

Liz, without whom things would have been a lot more difficult over the last couple of years. An outstanding assistant and friend, and one hell of a woman.

Nick Davies, who worked the Monmouth case with me. One of the most talented witches I've had the pleasure of knowing, and one who cuts through the bullshit with a glee that's all too rare in my experience of Wicca.

The rest of the people involved in the Monmouth case from chapter eight, for permission to use photographs and their real names. Special thanks to Tim Gunter for supplying extra photos and his account of the events that took place.

Lorna Russell, my editor, for translating my meanderings into English, and Robert Caskie, my agent, for making sure I didn't make too much of a fool out of myself.

Abi Silvester, for reading a number of versions of this thing, not getting too bored, and asking the questions I'm too used to this stuff to think of.

Finally I have to thank Diana, whose support, counsel and company made it possible for me to write this book. While this book wouldn't have happened without everyone I've mentioned (and several others), it was Diana who kept me going.

CONTENTS

INTRODUCTION

'So do you believe in all that, then?'

You'd be surprised how often people ask me that when they find out what I do. Although I do have an urge to slap them and ask if they'd ask a rat-catcher if he believed in rats, I give them a slightly non-plussed look, raise an eyebrow and give them an answer they're not expecting. The same answer I'm going to give you now, in fact, because if I'm going to spend the next few hundred pages talking about this I think it's best you know where I stand at the beginning.

I do believe that some people can't take a hint and hang around when they really should leave the party so someone else can get at the buffet table. I also believe that there are other non-physical entities that produce similar effects. In my experience, the latter are far more common. Both are dealt with in similar ways, although the technical details vary from case to case. This is why all the groups who deal with these problems have specialists to do so.

I am one of those specialists. My job is to make these things go away. I don't have to care what it is (beyond defining how to deal with it) or where it's going, or why it's there. All these things have to be secondary to me. I classify it, I define the best course of action and then I get rid of it. No matter how much sympathy I may feel, where the presence is malign my job is to remove that presence – either to relocate it elsewhere, or remove it entirely. I try to be as kind as I can to all parties involved, but at the end of the day I'm here to take care of the living.

So yeah, I believe that weird stuff happens. In twenty years as a magician I've seen and done things that defy so-called 'rational' explanation. I believe, however, that science will, in the end, explain this – ghosts, exorcism, magic, psychic powers and all the rest. Just because we can't explain a thing at the moment, it doesn't mean it isn't there.

There are those who seek to prove that these things are real. There are those who seek to prove they're not. There are those who just want an answer to the question 'What's next?' I am not a member of any of these groups. All I have to do is help someone – living, dead, somewhere in-between. We go in, we take care of business and we go home. Simple. Free of any agenda. Only the job in hand is important.

Mentioning agendas, I should be honest and tell you mine. As an exorcist, my point of view is considerably different from that of the people who normally write this sort of book. I have no need – or inclination – to prove or disprove the existence of ghosts, spooks, sprites, spirits, goblins, ghouls, vampires or honest politicians. My task is simply to determine whether or not the phenomenon in a certain location can be identified as a physical issue such as plumbing, or qualifies as non-physical. If it's in my purview, I determine the best way of removing it and do it as quickly as possible. I don't care if what's happening meets someone else's definition of 'real' – it's real enough for the purposes of getting the job done. All I want to do is remove whatever it is so the people involved can get on with their lives.

This book is about what has happened to me at work. Strange noises in the night, things that move by themselves, times and places and people that seem to ignore what we generally assume to be the rules by which the world works. I'm going to try to simply tell the tale, to explain what happened in these places and let you make your own mind up. The cases that follow are representative of those that I deal with regularly – a slice of my life. Classify these events any way you want but they happened to me. I was there. They happened in people's homes, their offices, their local pub, all the places where we live our day-to-day lives. No big houses on hilltops, no dry ice, and not much of a special effects budget, but these things remind us that the universe in which we live is wild and mad and scary, and the comfortable little places that we call home, where we feel safe, barely show us the surface of it.

I'm also going to talk a little about my opinions on the things I've seen, and my own theories about how and why these things happen. Let me stress this: my *opinions*. I don't claim to have all the answers, just a way of looking at things that accommodates what seems to be happening. I'm not always going to be polite, but I am going to be honest. If I think something is somebody's fault, I shall say so, and I'll try to give credit where it's due, too.

I'm also going to play a little fast and loose with language. Magic works on metaphor a lot of the time and I'm going to use a few terms here that will send respectable scientists reaching for large heavy objects with which to explain the error of my ways. If you hit a term that seems to mean something you're not sure about, check the back of the book where I've included a short glossary of terms and what they mean when I use them in this context. I've tried to keep this to a minimum, but there are a few points where conventional English staggers a little and I have to throw it a crutch.

I accepted the invitation to write this book to show what really happens. While I haven't seen the special effects you'd expect to see at the cinema, I have seen a pile of strange stuff. But what I hope to do here is let you see that we're fairly ordinary people who just happen to do an unusual job. We're here to help, just like so many other people that you see every day. While I hope you never need us, just remember that we, and a few others, are there if you do.

So when people ask if I believe in ghosts, they get an answer they weren't expecting, a smile and a quote from Shakespeare: 'There are more things in Heaven and Earth, Horatio, than are dreamt of in your philosophy.'

David Devereux

part one

WELCOME TO MY WORLD

chapter one

HELLO. MY NAME'S DAVID AND I'M AN EXORCIST

If you'd told me twenty years ago that I was going to be an exorcist when I grew up, my first reaction would have been either amusement or disbelief. Or maybe derision. But as I sit down to write this book, I've been studying magic for twenty years. Real magic, that is. What Aleister Crowley (one of the fathers of modern magical theory and certainly the most famous and the most controversial) referred to as 'The changing of reality in accordance with will'. Not card tricks, although I was pretty keen on those when I was younger and still enjoy watching a prestidigitator or illusionist display their skills. No, I mean your actual magic – sorcery, thaumaturgy, call it what you will. The spooky stuff that most people associate with devil worship and movies with too much dry ice in them. But if you told that thirteen-year-old boy what he'd be doing come the twenty-first century, he'd have mocked you and told you he planned to go and work in the City as a trader on the stock market. A few years later he'd have told you he was going to be a solicitor, as a local practice had planned to send him up to Oxford to study law. Later, a computer geek, or a soldier. But not, strangely enough, a professional consulting magician specialising in paranormal problems.

But, at the age of thirty-four, that's exactly what I do.

I've been in this particular area for a few years now, having started helping people occasionally. A few years ago, a close friend started a company named Athanor Consulting – a company that now advises clients worldwide on how to deal with curses, hauntings, and all the other sorts of paranormal oddness that have been getting a lot more common over the last few years as well as providing a consultancy and technical advisory service for people writing about the subject with no background who wanted to get it right. We're by no means the most famous group dealing with these things but we're generally considered to be pretty good at what we do and have well-known clients who appreciate our policy of discretion.

Why do I say it's been getting more common? Certainly the media are more comfortable reporting it and there are now several more magazines reporting on inexplicable and paranormal events than there were even five years ago. More relevantly to me, people seem a lot more comfortable talking about these things. It may be that things like this have been happening at a constant level but are now more frequently reported or that more events are happening. I know that I see and hear about more cases now than I ever have before and I think that there are more things happening, since people have rarely been shy about telling me their ghost stories.

At Athanor, I hold the title 'Senior Field Officer'. What this means, in essence, is that I'm number two in the company and involved in the more interesting cases that we deal with. I specialise in curse removal and the elimination of non-physical entities and provide advice to clients and colleagues on other matters.

But that's not all. I also lecture, write radio comedy scripts, enjoy cookery, clubbing, real ale, reading, the songs of Noël Coward, heavy drinking, cinema, wild parties, modern and classical art and walking. This is just to show that I'm a reasonably well-rounded human being, albeit one who's hopeless at relationships.

So how did I get here?

I was born in late 1971 not far from the town in Cornwall where I grew up (but not on a dark and stormy night, I'm told it was really quite clement – no portents here). My home life was a happy one, my family loving and supportive. I grew up with a love of vintage jazz music and old stories and preferred the company of adults – as many bright children do. I was by nature a fairly solitary child (although I talked a lot given an audience – some things never change), and was bullied at school pretty much from the day I got there. Kind of a yin-yang deal, I suppose you could say – great home, bloody awful school.

But in other ways, it was a great place to be a kid. There was stuff around for me to do, places for me to discover, cliffs I could walk for miles and adults who were willing to put up with the smart kid. This is the way I learned concepts like honour, loyalty and not hitting someone you really don't have to. I had one hellacious temper back then, though – which didn't show often. Of course, when it did, it scared me. I was eleven when I really lost it – the real 'red mist' experience. It ended up with a kid being taken to the local hospital. While it was forgiven and forgotten, it left a major mark on me – the price of losing control. I decided not to do it again. So at the age of eleven I learned one of the skills that is still invaluable to me today – the ability to switch off my emotions and worry about the situation afterwards. I'm fairly sure that most psychologists will agree that this isn't really a healthy thing to do and I don't do it unless it's strictly necessary. As an example of this, I performed as a stand-up comedian during my twenties and suffered from really awful stage fright –

almost to the point of vomiting. It never occurred to me to switch that off. It's a trick I use only when safety becomes an issue. Firstly, it removes you from the experience; secondly, it makes it difficult for other people to deal with you (imagine being at a party with Mr Spock) and thirdly, the comedown's a *bitch*.

I was thirteen when I started to take an interest in the paranormal. I'd taken a summer job helping with luggage on the bus service between my hometown and the rail link at Exeter and this gave me extra cash and access to much bigger bookshops. It was a revelation in so many ways, but one day I picked up a copy of Dion Fortune's book *Psychic Self Defence* (one I recommend even now – see the 'recommended reading' at the back of the book), read it and felt my interest take a whole new direction. It is, to me, a great thing to be able to say that my mother did not freak out when I told her. She told me to be careful, but supported me in the idea that I had to find out my own truths for myself – and this is the same woman who insisted I went to Sunday School every week until I was old enough to make an informed decision for myself whether I wanted to attend or not because she made a promise to God and took it seriously.

I suppose there are many theories that could be put forward about why I was attracted to this area of study. Let's give everyone a thrill and say I wanted the power I thought it promised. I was bullied, teased – treated as if I was at the bottom of the food chain. I was the smart, fat kid with glasses – the one nobody wanted to be friends with. I had a few friends, but not many. I wasn't popular, I didn't get round to having a girlfriend until I left school. I was an outsider, a loner, and wanted something of my own that didn't rely on anyone else for validation or status. So I found a field that intrigued me – one that worked because of my mind, one that worked when I got stuff right and didn't when I got stuff wrong. I have since learned that this is the mindset of a computer hacker and that's a very close model to what I had started to become. A reality hacker. Years later, it was fascinating to read the *Hacker Manifesto* and see the parallels between the way I came to the occult and the way that the classic hacker finds computers. Perhaps if we'd had a modem for my computer at home I'd be writing a book about computers now.

But the truth is that I can't remember why I started. It looked interesting, different – and it was sufficiently different to be sure that I wouldn't suddenly find an entire cabal in the common room looking down their noses at me.

Once I'd read that first book, I decided to find out more. I met a chap who was practising and teaching crystal healing in Exeter and persuaded him to let me hang around and learn stuff. I can't say for sure how much he was humouring me, but it was enough to convince me that I was living in a much wider world than I'd previously thought. So I started to read more. What money I made was spent on books about magic – starting with Dion Fortune again (she made sense to me) and her system of magic based on Greek mythology. From there, the floodgates opened.

I started to read whatever I could. I became a frequent visitor to my local library, ordering whatever books I could. One would, inevitably, lead to another, and another. I understand that at some point the librarian had a quiet word with my folks about my taste in learning materials and was told that things were OK and I had permission to read pretty much whatever I wanted. By the age of fifteen I knew a fair amount and was working with the mental disciplines that allowed me to go further still. Since the school victim wasn't going to get an education in matters relating to girls, I found something else to occupy my energies.

One thing I discovered was that the teachings and philosophies of the New Age were not for me. While I am a great believer in peace, and living in harmony with the rest of the world, I realised early on (perhaps thanks to those kids who were bullying me) that universal peace and love are still a fair way off, given the current evolutionary state of the human race. I was definitely going to be approaching this with the Old School attitude. I realised also that all the extra capabilities that come with study come with a price tag, be it in blood, sweat, or tears. We are the sum of all our experiences, the bad times are as important as the good and life as a magician comes with all of these things. It was a hell of a thing for a fifteen-year-old to discover and, while I can't say I like it even now, it's still the basis of my personal philosophy.

I am reminded of the story of a farmer in ancient China. One day, his horse ran away. All his neighbours gathered round to comfort him – 'What a terrible thing!' they said. But the farmer was quiet and thoughtful. 'How do you know?' he asked. Well, a couple of weeks passed, and his horse came back, accompanied by seven others including a fine wild stallion. His neighbours rejoiced, 'What a wonderful thing! Such fortune!' but the farmer was still quiet. He looked at his neighbours as they smiled and clapped him on the back and asked quietly 'How do you know?' As you'd expect, the farmer kept the horses and his son began breaking in the stallion and in the process managed to break his leg. There was wailing and sympathy for the farmer, but his only response was 'How do you know this is bad?' Well, this was a troubled time in China and the army came through to levy troops. All the young men of the village were taken to be soldiers in the Emperor's army – except the boy with the broken leg. Once again, the farmer was congratulated on his great good fortune at still having his son to help him. But the farmer, realising his neighbours would never understand, shook his head and asked...

Well, anyway.

So, while it wasn't an easy process learning my trade (a process that I can assure you is still continuing), I learned early on that you either take the whole package or you go home. What I do know is that I wouldn't swap it for the world.

After a couple of years, I realised that it was time to stop sitting on the fence and actually get on with it. I could either be an occultist and spend my life reading lots of theory, or I could be a magician and actually put what I was learning into practice. I wanted something that wouldn't do any damage and since it was a dry week with no rain predicted for a few days I thought I'd try to make it rain the next day.

I unpacked all the kit I thought I'd need, had candles burning, family out for the evening, drew strange symbols all over the place and chanted like a good 'un. There was a shiver down my spine as I finished, and I had a sudden urge to clear everything away and forget all about it. I followed the urge and could hardly sleep come bedtime, since I'd managed to scare myself silly.

But if that was scary, then you should have seen me the next morning when I awoke to the sound of rain hammering down outside.

All the magicians I know have a moment where they suddenly realise that magic works. It's a major thing and it changes your life. I didn't want to believe that I'd caused the rainstorm, but the fact that it lasted a day (as requested), and occurred over a pretty localised area was more than a little convincing. By that age I knew not to bother trusting the weather forecast, even though it said 'Sunny' and that was how it was for the rest of the week. Was it a coincidence, or was it magic? Much as I wanted it to be the former, I felt that I had to conclude it was the latter.

I suppose you're wondering if I used my new skills to get back at the bullies. I didn't. Not once. That moment of clarity after the red mist had taught me well. I never let myself get angry enough to hit anyone straight off. I'm more likely to walk off, think about it and then come back and hit you twice as hard once I'm sure you deserve it. But I wouldn't have gone after my fellow school kids with this stuff – just as I wouldn't have gone after them with a shotgun. Even a couple of years ago when a couple of kids wrapped a brandy bottle around my face, my first thought was 'What sort of life do they have that this is the only way they can express themselves?' and, despite several offers from people willing to explain the error of their ways, I stayed those hands and have left those children – for that's all they really were – to get on with their lives. Not only that, I feel that revenge is a bad habit. Once you decide that the world is responsible for all your problems you give up a great deal of power over your own life and if you start trying to get back at the world all you do is hurt a load of innocent people. In the end, though, the only person you really end up hurting is yourself.

This is the way things continued as life went on through the nineties. I studied, I travelled, and I learned a lot. I discovered the Western Esoteric Tradition – most famously practised by the Golden Dawn and suchlike with heavy influences from ancient Egypt and theories of Atlantis. I read books on the subject that had been written centuries ago (and are now available in regular bookstores) then on to more exotic ideas. I found a great deal in Tibetan shamanism worth recommending, if you can stand the pace. The same can be said for the Vodou religion, which has grown from its West

African roots to provide a powerful and practical system of magic as part of its theology. I also studied the ancient Chinese systems aligned with Taoism, the Wiccan revival of Gerald Gardner and Aleister Crowley (especially with Sanders' later developments) and more modern forms such as Chaos Magic and Technomancy. I even managed to find time to play a pretty good hand of poker (a more useful life skill than many people realise, although one that can occasionally lead to problems). There were periods where I took a break, letting things rearrange themselves in my head. There was also a lot of work, and I learned a great deal. It was not, of course, without cost. I have, as a result of the life I have chosen, known heartbreak, and disability, and horror, and terror, and loneliness. I've come close to losing my mind more than once and have found myself doing things that seem in retrospect to have been so astonishingly stupid that it's a wonder that I'm still alive and moderately sane. But I have also known joy, and love, and seen things so full of wonder as to make your heart break at the memory of them. It's certainly been a whole lot of life for a fellow my age.

Of course, I still needed to eat and that led me to an interesting succession of jobs that could only have ended up with me writing a book. I worked in technical support (which taught me a lot about problem-solving and how stupid people can be when taken out of where they're in control). I sold timeshare (which taught me how to manipulate the truth in ways I'm not very proud of), then advertising (which taught me whole new levels of outright lying and that standing on a chair while trying to talk to someone on the phone makes me feel stupid). I flipped burgers for a short while (which taught me a great deal about racism, but not in the way I expected), I sang jazz, I played some serious poker (which taught me an awful lot about an awful lot) and even worked in a mortuary.

It was in the nineties that I first came across the concept of the multimodel approach to magic generally known as Chaos. The strange thing about all the studies I'd pursued with a wide variety of people was that, while nobody had a problem teaching me stuff, nobody seemed to want me as a permanent fixture of their group, either. So, I'd had no ties to prevent me from moving on to learn something else (a situation that contributed to a very nasty break-up from a witch who I was involved with for a brief while – she really didn't approve). So I was happy to move along every so often, learning a lot, keeping the bits that worked for me and discarding those that didn't. Then I heard of Bruce Lee, arguably the greatest martial artist of the twentieth century. He'd done the same thing with his studies and created a way of fighting that worked specifically the way he did. I thought about Crowley and the way he'd studied a number of styles before working out what worked for him. So I applied both of these examples to the multimodel school and by jingo – *it all made sense!*

So, I can hear you shouting from here – what is this multimodel thing I'm wittering on about? This is the bit where I talk about magic. Because, in the way I work, an exorcism is just another magical operation. It's the way I learned to do it and forms the basic foundation of what's to come.

So let's start with how I think magic works. This is one of several theories, none of which can be proven at this time. I don't know if my theory's right, but it seems to fit what few scientific facts there are, as well as my moral and metaphysical view of the universe. Many people will disagree with me – I'm expecting that and expect to get into arguments about it occasionally.

Imagine, if you will, that I'm wearing brown robes, sitting in a desert and trying to explain to you about a universal life force that binds all living things together. This is the basic principle of the Taoist religion: one universe in a dance of balance between two forms of energy – Yin and Yang. Light and dark, birth and death, peanut butter and jelly – all things are part of the great Tao, and that which can be defined as the Tao is by its very nature not the Tao. From the great dance comes energy, which the Taoists call Chi, and Chi is very interesting stuff. Everything contains Chi – from the smallest rock to the greatest whale. It is in the food we eat, and the air we breathe – is any of this starting to sound familiar yet? This energy can be harnessed and this is how we get to see little old guys throw seven-foot behemoths around like rag dolls. Once you start working with Chi, it stops being about muscle and starts being about energy.

As far as I'm concerned, magic works the same way.

I don't believe in a great good energy, or a great dark energy, or a particular consciousness driving either. I don't believe that magic comes from the devil, or from God, or His angels, or His Great Aunt Agatha. It's a means of harnessing energy, just like the great wizards who can harness the power of the great sky god's wrath and use it to light the box of demons who dance and sing for me – sorry, just like electricity. Now electricity can power my box of demons – television – quite easily, or it can power a life-support machine, or an electric chair, or a car that doesn't use fossil fuels to get about. It's neutral in and of itself. It's when you start messing around with it that you start hitting moral issues. In this same way, I can use magic to heal, to harm, to show a young lady a particularly entertaining time or to deal with non-physical entities. Telling me I'm evil because I'm able to relieve somebody's pain for a while is the same as telling a doctor that she's evil for allowing a patient any other form of pain relief.

Let's go back to Bruce Lee for a moment. Pretty much everybody has heard of Bruce Lee. Bruce's life's work was summed up in a book published by his wife after his death called *The Tao of Jeet Kune Do*, or *The Way of The Way of the Intercepting Fist*. What this has been assumed to be about by most people – who've looked at the drawings and notes on technique – is a new style of fighting culled from the many systems that Bruce Lee studied and became proficient in.

It isn't.

What the book IS about, and this is stated very clearly in the philosophical sections, is approach – not being constrained by systems that do not work for you, not being held in thought patterns that are bad for you purely because they belong to a system that otherwise works, not continuing to perform a technique that has no useful application in the twenty-first century just because it is required for your next belt.

The book is about creating a system of fighting that makes best use of your mind and body, cutting away techniques that have no use for you and adopting those that do. What this book tells us is that we are all different and it is foolish to expect one set of techniques to work for everybody. After all, I may practice Tai Chi, but my body size and shape – let alone my diet and activity schedule – are somewhat different from a Taoist monk's.

The most famous man to take this approach with magic was Aleister Crowley, and I'm willing to bet you've heard of him, too...

Crowley, who I have already referred to as one of the founding fathers of modern magic, was a notorious figure during the first decades of the twentieth century. Known as 'The wickedest man in the world', and 'The Great Beast of Revelation', he was a chess champion, an expert mountaineer, a mystic, a sexual revolutionary and a magician of some skill.

He studied widely in many parts of the world, and finally created the Thelemic style of magic, which he propagated through his organisation the Ordo Templi Orientis. Personally I have a great deal of respect for his approach and for his introduction of scientific materialism to the practice of magic. The practical result of his wide base of study was to give him a viewpoint that transcended pretty much every other magician on the planet – and he used it. He assembled a system of magic that worked for him. He recorded this and made it available to others, in much the way that Bruce Lee did. And all was well.

Where Crowley and Lee part company and where I feel Crowley went wrong, is that he solidified. His truth was The Truth, inviolable and right beyond argument – the final, absolute form of the art and science of magic to be studied and propagated, replacing all other forms.

I think most of the magicians I know would disagree with that view, although their reasons may vary somewhat. However, the reason I, and the multimodel movement as a whole, disagree is that I hold very few opinions that are considered absolute. Cars are solid, but ideas are not. The art of this approach is to be able to believe something completely, absolutely and passionately for five minutes, then change to whichever belief is required for the next operation. So, while I may presently choose to believe that vodka is my friend, Angelina Jolie is cute and Paul Smith makes great suits, all these beliefs are subject to change as a matter of practicality. Especially the one about vodka.

What we come to, in effect, is a meta-belief that belief itself is the force that drives our magic and, through changes in our own belief structures, we can use the most effective technique for the task we wish to address.

Let's try that again, without the esoteric bullshit.

Simply put, what I and my colleagues seek is an understanding of the basic techniques of magic – the blocks, kicks, punches and so on – looking beneath the varying styles we have studied to find the basic points of correlation. What we seek is not chaos, but the underlying order within the seemingly chaotic that allows all of us to do what we do. We seek the mechanisms behind the psychodrama, the elements normally referred to in metaphor and guarded language – the source code, if you will. We want to look behind the masks worn by the gods and see what lies beneath. What we seek are the foundations of magic.

As anyone who has tried or read about more than one style of ritual will tell you, magical rituals tend to be pretty similar across the various geographical, cultural and temporal boundaries. Most temples, halls, circles, covens and crews use almost identical tools and techniques to get the job done; it's just a question of language and which deific forms are used.

In magic, as far as I and many others are concerned, ritual serves only one purpose – to allow the participants to achieve a state in which they believe totally that magic is real, possible, and will work. Hence, whatever gets you to that state is valid. There are those who prefer a five-hour ritual, there are those who follow the shamanistic mode with hallucinogens, there are those, like myself, who use meditation – with or without external influences – and sex magic is always a popular one. What you use is, in my opinion, irrelevant. The destination is important, not the route you take to get there. Personally, I like to use technology to assist me – recorded music, imagery, brainwave modulators or any other tool that I feel will aid the task in hand. The trick, of course, is being able to do this without laptop, personal stereo, cute girlie or whatever. As a friend of mine – Nick the Witch, who you'll meet in chapter twelve – is fond of saying, 'Anyone can feel magical in a ritual robe, but if you can't do magic in just a pair of soiled underpants then you ain't worth shit!'

The Chaos 'style' has been ill served by what I call 'Leather Trench-coats', in the same way that Wicca (modern Witchcraft) has been by what some call the 'Wannablessedbes', people who like the *idea* of being a witch or a magician but don't necessarily have the dedication or ability to learn how to do it properly. To do any form of magic takes practice, hard work and time, and this is no exception. Reading a book by Phil Hine, putting on some black leather and stalking around saying 'I'm a Chaos Magician!' has the same effect as reading something in a bad book on Wicca and thinking you're qualified to run a coven. One book of spells does not a magician make and while raw natural talent can take you a certain distance, it's training and practice that make the difference. People like that have done a lot of damage to the relationship between the traditional community and those of us out on the fringes, to the point where I face my first visit to a new pagan moot with some trepidation. But every field of study has its share of assholes and the esoteric world is no different from the mundane in that respect.

The one thing our end of things tends not to have is those who sit in the middle ground, or on the fence. In this field, you're either serious or a wanker. People in the multimodel school invoke anyone from the Goddess to Great Cthulhu and, while true followers may get cut a little slack, we don't, because many deities have a tendency to get jealous. This is not a methodology for everyone. It does not provide a vehicle for spiritual fulfilment (we seek that elsewhere), but what it can provide is results. There are no compromises and it is by no means easy. Control while working has to be absolute, especially when working with others, and the level of flexibility it provides is a result of the extra work that is involved behind the scenes in study and research. Discipline is paramount and is in some cases the only tool that ensures survival when things get interesting.

How all this applies to 'ghost busting' (and since I hate that term it's the only time you're going to see it in the whole book) will be explained in the next chapter.

The reason I've explained all this to you now is simple. I expect that most of the people who buy this book will not have a background in magic or the occult and, even among those who do, there's no way for me to tell how many of you might have come across my field of practice before. So I want to try and put our case as clearly as possible. I should also say that I don't necessarily feel that the path of any tradition is necessarily invalid. The traditions provide a useful framework for a practitioner to understand what we do. This is merely the method that works for me today. There is nothing to say that I may wake up tomorrow and become a full-time Wiccan, or Christian, or Scientologist (did you know, by the way, that they won't take anyone with magical training?). My methods, and my current faith in them, are not necessarily right, but they work for me.

Magic has been called an art – sometimes the Great Art. It's also been called a science. Sometimes it gets called both, especially when I'm on my soapbox. I realise that this isn't what you'd expect to read in a book of this type, but I suppose that's because this is a different type of book – one written by somebody who does this for a living. I am certainly different from the people one generally associates with this sort of activity in that, while I might admit to a certain level of psychic talent and certainly have some skills in that area, I'd never claim to be a medium. That doesn't mean I don't believe mediums exist, quite the opposite in fact. It just means that I'm not one, any more than the average medium can do what I do. I'm also useless with engines, plumbing and other forms of DIY. I can programme the clock on my VCR, though, so I hope I'm not a total loss.

chapter two

BASIC PRINCIPLES OF EXORCISM

Exorcists are, as a rule, a quiet bunch. We don't talk about what we do. It's not that we're particularly secretive, although confidentiality is very important. Mostly it's because people really don't want to know. Most people just aren't equipped to deal with things outside their regular terms of reference. When you get far enough from the standard precepts of someone's reality they literally won't see what's happening. It's how the brain defends itself. A massive change in world-view isn't necessarily healthy so if you only come across one flying pink elephant in your life, the odds are you'll fail to notice it, or decide it's a balloon, or come up with an explanation that fits the facts closely enough to allow you to forget all about it. Forgetting all about it is good.

We magicians train to open our awareness to allow us to see things like this[1] and deal with them. It's why some people find us a little odd – you tell us that the sky's pink and we'll consider the idea for a second. To us, there are various options. You might be seeing light refracted from a different angle, one of us might have a different eye structure from the

[1] Although I personally *haven't* seen any flying pink elephants. Or at least I don't remember seeing them if I have.

other, one of might be experiencing (ahem) an altered state of consciousness, or you might be talking rubbish. But we're not going to leap straight to option four just because we suppose that the sky is blue and we can't deal with the idea that we might be wrong. It would be foolish to close off all those possibilities because of an assumption.

The basic principles I am going to discuss here are the ones that apply to the way I work. I will not claim that they are the only ones that work, because there are fine people working in other systems who do a perfectly good job using entirely different methods. I do not consider it appropriate for *anyone* to stand up and say, 'My way is right. Your way is wrong. Your failure to believe in my magical system/deity of choice/lifestyle invalidates your opinion!' There are those who do consider it a reasonable course of action – who actually use threats, and acts, of violence to try and make their point. I believe that to be wrong, and will have no part of it.

Before I go on to tell you about exorcism, here's a brief message from the lawyers: DON'T TRY THIS AT HOME, KIDS! It's dangerous. I'm going to assume that nobody reading this is stupid enough to think that reading a process overview and a few accounts of field-work qualifies you for life as a member of my profession. If anybody does – go back and read the previous chapter again. Think about it. Consider everything I've been through and learned to get me where I am. Compare it to your own life. If you can honestly say that your biography contains as much study, as much experience and as many difficult moments IN THIS FIELD as mine, then consider studying the subject. But don't think that this book is a 'how-to', because it isn't – any more than watching a war film qualifies you as an army commander.

So, let's talk about exorcism. The process I detail hereafter is the one we use at Athanor, which works best for us.

Preparation is your friend. Everything we do starts with research. When we first hear from a client, they give us varying amounts of information and in as many ways as there are clients. Thus we have a standard questionnaire (which I have included at the end of this chapter), which is sent to all potential clients as we are evaluating their case. It's worth noting that we don't automatically accept all the cases brought to us for many reasons, be they physical (such as we think a plumber would fix the problem more effectively), medical (frequently relating to mental health) or psychic (something feels wrong and we're not happy to intervene in that particular situation) – and the first phase of dealing with a new client involves both parties looking at the situation and each other and deciding if we can work together. Sometimes one side or the other will decide that it's not appropriate for us to deal with the problem, and we go our separate ways.

Assuming that we're taking the case, we look at the questionnaire. Then we come up with more questions and these are forwarded to the client. The more detail that can be gained before getting to the site, the better. The value of good research cannot be overstated – it allows one to build a picture of what's been happening to lead the client to contact Athanor in the first place and means that when we reach the site we're prepared for the possible consequences of our arrival.

As you might reasonably suppose, safety is paramount. Both for the team, and the client.

Alongside the client questionnaires, researching the area is also important. I am lucky to have colleagues with a wide range of knowledge about the British Isles – everything from local history to sacred sites (of all flavours) and areas of traditional supernatural activity. It can be very useful to have advance knowledge that the place you're about to visit is right in the middle of a traditional faerie route, for example, as it can suggest possible causes to be investigated on site.

Research is the longest part of the process as long as the client is not in danger. Once the research has been done, an appointment is arranged for us to visit the client, all contact having taken place thus far by telephone and email. A standard Athanor field team consists of three members – all trained to handle the situation individually – working in a loose formation that allows the most qualified person to take charge as the process flows. Ego is a useful tool in magical operations, but as with any other team it has no place when we're working together. This flexibility is one of our primary strengths and allows us to work effectively in a much wider variety of situations than some others in the field.

Flexibility is, to be honest, possibly the thing we're proudest of developing at Athanor. It's the thing that sets us apart from many other practitioners in this field. Flexibility of style and approach and of operating hierarchy allows us to work together in high-stress situations with the speed and accuracy necessary to get the job done as quickly and effectively as possible.

Anyway, back to the meeting. We make a point of dressing like professionals of any other type when possible – suits and such under most circumstances – rather than having any kind of 'new age' look about us. We feel that this helps to reassure the client. After all, they've engaged professional assistance, so it isn't too much to ask us to look like it. In a field where belief is as vital as it is here, it is imperative that the client has absolute trust in us. Everything is set to make that as easy as possible. Having engaged us, there is quite frequently a part of a client's mind that asks themselves if they are doing the right thing, so we endeavour to make them as comfortable as possible around us. The client is then interviewed, using the data already gathered to ascertain any final details that will help us. Extensive use is made of body language and linguistic analysis at the same time, to give us as full a picture as possible of the client's state of physical and mental health. Though we are not mental health professionals, we can estimate the level of stress a client is experiencing and treat them accordingly. It's rather like poker: if you want to win the occasional hand you have to learn to watch the other players carefully. You're looking for 'tells', those little signals that can quite literally give the game away when someone's bluffing, or when they have a good hand, or whatever else. These things tell much more than words and that's what I'm looking for. My interest lies in what the client isn't telling us as much as what they are: their actual emotional state, how well they seem to have been eating and sleeping, and a range of other little details that can provide information that might come in useful later when it's all put together to form a complete picture.

It is most common that one member of the three-person team is adept at dealing with the client as the other two work – allowing brief technical conversations to be explained so that there is no feeling of exclusion. We work *with* a client and cannot do our jobs without their complete co-operation. Where we are obstructed, or where unreasonable conditions are placed upon our operations, we have to withdraw, as we cannot predict a reasonable chance of success and this inevitably leads to bad feeling on both sides.

During the interview, one member of the team is on lookout duty, watching the environment for changes that may indicate the beginnings of resistance from whatever might be there. Temperature changes, profound emotional responses... Many reactions are possible and need to be watched for with an eye not involved in the actual interview.

Finally, we reach stage three of the pre-action phase – the site walk. This is where the sensitivity of the team needs to be at its height. As a group, we systematically investigate the whole site, trying to find anything that seems wrong in any sense at all. Copious photographs are taken, along with video footage. As a member of the team picks something up, it's flagged to everyone else and noted for discussion at the end. Examples run across quite a range – temperature fluctuation is a well-known effect, along with shadows that don't quite 'fit'. It is also important to watch for the things you'd expect – unusual animal behaviour, sounds, children and so on. The more data that can be collected, the better.

This phase of the operation ends with a meeting. We take everything we've observed, from the first contact with the client to the beginning of the meeting itself, and discuss it. What we're trying to do here is classify exactly what we think is going on. As a rule, we normally agree about these sort of things very quickly – we have the data and the background knowledge – so conclusions tend to follow with equal speed. With that decision, the investigation phase comes to a nominal end and we enter the active phase of the assignment. Where we hold the meeting varies from case to case, but we try to avoid doing it in front of a client wherever possible purely because the slang flies thick and fast, and were the client present we'd either have to waste time explaining every other word or insult them by talking over their head.

It is worth mentioning here, and not for the last time, that a great many of such cases can be solved without resorting to aggressive measures. When one is dealing with the dead, it tends to be a matter of pointing this out to the entity, who most probably hasn't actually noticed that they've died and is quite ready to get on with far more interesting things once you make it clear that there's an entire universe of possibilities out there for them.

This isn't always easy, I admit – and sometimes they prefer to stay and peacefully coexist with the current residents of a place – but in my experience it's the most common outcome.

Once we reach the active phase, things speed up quite significantly. We prefer not to allow an entity time to react, or marshal defences, or start attacking first. As a result of this, most outside observers would probably tell you that this is where things start getting exciting.

The first decision to be taken is about the desired end result. If we're dealing with a benign entity then our preferred outcome is merely to move them on, or explain that they're causing distress and persuade them to stop it. It's worth remembering here that many families actually quite like the idea of having a friendly presence in the house and children find a particular talent for relating to them, particularly to entities of a more maternal character (although of course if it's friendly we're unlikely to have been called in to take a look). If, on the other hand, we have determined the presence to be hostile we have more options. Depending on circumstance, we may look to trap it within another item for removal and safe storage (think 'Genie in a bottle'), we may look to provide a gate for it to return where it came from, or to a more suitable dimension. In extreme cases, we would consider complete eradication. While not exactly a simple process, there are times when such action is the only manner by which we can guarantee client safety.

Once we know what we want as a result, we start considering ways and means. From the gentlest negotiating tactics to the fiercest styles of magical and psychic combat, we attempt to use the minimum amount of force that gets the job done – this is both for our own benefit and for the client, as we don't want to leave any more residue to be cleaned up than strictly necessary.

This seems like a good time to stop for a moment to explain what an exorcism actually is and, just as importantly, what it isn't. The process I refer to here as exorcism has any number of names, depending on whom you ask. I have chosen to use the Christian term on the grounds that it is easily recognised by the general populace, and likewise describe myself as an exorcist. I have been described in one magazine as a Demon Slayer, for example. So the process can also be described as deliverance, or cleansing, or space clearing, or any other of a wide variety of terms. What we're talking about is the removal of a non-physical influence or entity from a place or person by means of a magical process. For these purposes, I am classifying religious variations of this same process as magic also. Whether the effects come about as a result of divine intervention or the focusing of my own will and energies is a fascinating argument, but one that has no place here.

The process begins with protection for all persons involved. Generally this is taken care of for an Athanor team before we even get to the site, but I understand that some people prefer to leave it somewhat later. Good psychic shielding is, in my opinion, a necessary skill for daily life in the twenty-first century, but the level to which a professional in this field must be protected is an order of magnitude beyond that. Once the process has begun, an antipathetic entity is going to take any steps it can to protect itself from the removal process. This can start with something as simple as feelings of unease and can manifest in such physical effects as objects moving at speed and direct attempts to harm and possess members of the team or client group. As you might expect, protection of the client group is paramount. It is safe to assume that they will have little or no magical experience, let alone in the rather specialised field of magical combat, so an important part of the team's job is to maintain their safety at all times. At Athanor, a member of the team generally sits with the group, allowing them to hear an explanation of the process as it happens, thus ensuring that an adequate shielding level is held at all times. With that taken care of, the rest of the team can get on with the job.

Having identified the cause of the trouble during the investigation phase, the team will already have a pretty good idea of what's to be done – part of the flexibility of the multimodel system is that it provides us with options and we can tailor those options to deal with each case most effectively. The team leader will decide on the actual plan after discussion with the team and assign roles. As with any other team, we have specialisations as well as our general skills, and assignments tend to follow that pattern.

So we have a plan. Our clients are safe. We've got a problem, and a team to solve it. Time to get on with it, then. (Readers with any kind of magical background are going to start noticing a familiar pattern here. After all, magic's magic as far as I'm concerned and the similarity in underlying principles is what gives the multimodel school its attraction to me.)

We start by raising energy in ourselves – making sure the batteries are charged. We assume every time that we've got a rough time ahead of us, so pleasant surprises are more frequent than unpleasant ones. Each of us has a preferred method of doing this, and again some are time-dependent. So we pick whichever we have time for. With the batteries charged, we can start the job itself.

I'm going to cover some of the techniques we use in the case studies later but briefly what happens next is target acquisition. We have to find the seat of the activity (or the entity if it's mobile) and contain it. This is not as easy as it sounds. If you have a thing that is bound to a particular place, item or person, then you know where it is and all is well. If, on the other hand, it is mobile and has identified our intentions, then the hunt is on. It's worth remembering that, as far as the entity is concerned, it's effectively fleeing for its life but I don't care about that. Our job is to find the easiest resolution for all parties (including the entity if possible), but if a thing has to go, then a thing has to go. I don't have any moral difficulties with that.

So you track it down and you corner it. Then you secure the area to ensure it's not going anywhere. Then you do whatever has been decided.

If the decision has been made to trap it, then the area is made utterly inhospitable in such a way that, when the chance of escape (into the container or in some cases out through a temporary gateway) becomes available, the entity goes swiftly of its own accord. Alternatively, one tightens the containment again and again until the containment field itself can be mapped into the physical object chosen to act as a securing medium. Think of it as either throwing in a tear gas grenade then opening a door for the target to get out in the way you want, or shoving the target through the door with riot shields.

The least favourite choice, but one that is sometimes sadly necessary, is the termination of the entity. This is done as quickly and painlessly as possible. While a number of schools have grown up across the world that discuss and have developed methods of performing this particular function, I personally find Tibetan methods to be the most frequently effective.

I am sure that there are those who will question my ethics and will judge that my position in this matter renders anything else I have to say invalid. It's something I have become used to. I don't know if everything I deal with has feelings, and I don't always care because that's not my job. I'm enough of a softy to try to be as gentle as I can but for some people that's not good enough. To those people who would judge my policies, I ask a simple question: Would you blame a man who shot a mad dog?

What I'm trying to say is that this is not an easy job. It's a hard life, for hard people. I don't think of myself as your classic 'hard man', although I've studied a little of the martial arts and been through some tense times, but one gains a certain emotional resilience that helps one do the job. I don't enjoy destroying any form of life (or otherwise), to the point where I would rather move a bothersome insect from my home than kill it but in my job it isn't done for fun, it's done from necessity.

Once that's done, we walk the site again, keeping an open mind about the apparent success (or otherwise) of the actions taken. We basically search anew for any signs of paranormal or otherwise related activity and, if we catch anything we'd missed previously, start again. Once we've started, we like to have the job done in one visit, as this minimises the stress placed on the client. Not only that, this process is *tiring*. Once we've gone home and hit the sack, we need to sleep; the prospect of having to get out of bed in the morning to do it all over again doesn't appeal.

We'll assume in this case that everything went well. So, after we've declared the site to be clear, the process of after-care begins. If circumstances allow, we like to sit down and have a cup of tea with the client. The charging clock stops at this point, to encourage people to talk to us. We explain what's just happened, from our diagnosis of the problem through to the steps we took to take care of it. Then we'll happily talk about anything else. This gives us an opportunity to monitor the area and the client and, if everything has gone to plan, the relaxation one notices in both can be quite remarkable. The other factor is to ensure that clients see us as people and will then feel more comfortable about coming back to us if they need to.

We like to keep in touch with our clients after that actual job for a while, just to be sure that everything's OK. It does us no good to leave unhappy people behind us, even when the situation's been brought about by their lack of co-operation. Not only is it bad PR – not a good thing when most of your PR is by word of mouth – but it makes us unhappy. We take a great deal of pride in what we do and want to be sure that we do as god a job as we can. When that level of personal commitment starts to fade, then it becomes time to seriously rethink the direction of what we do.

When we leave it is generally with cheery waves and the happiness that comes from knowing we've been able to help someone who felt they had no place left to turn. A lot of our clients are desperate when they come to us – hardly a surprise in these modern times. For someone to say, 'I appear to need an exorcist to make my home habitable' is quite a leap in these days of science and scepticism and I admire the courage of those people who can since it takes a shift of world-view that many are not prepared to risk. The sad part of this tale is that for every person who contacts us there's another who keeps on rationalising it away until it destroys their lives, their relationships and everything else about them. I'm not saying there's no such thing as bad luck, but I wouldn't be comfortable using that as a catch-all excuse if my life started going comprehensively down the toilet without at least considering other possibilities. Fortunately, as these things are becoming easier to talk about and more commonly reported, people are finding it easier to come out and ask for help. It's not unlikely that someone you know will have had some kind of experience, or even that they might have called for some kind of help.

In the event of a recurrence, the client is warned to let us know as soon as they can. We have protocols to deal with this and the sooner we can start the sooner we can sort it out. As soon as we know of any worries, we arrange for a member of the team with remote viewing skills to examine the site psychically from a distance at the first opportunity. If caught quickly enough, clean-up work can be done at range using standard magical processes – we've only just left the place and we've become pretty familiar with it, so actually getting a magical operation organised effectively really isn't too much of a challenge. If we're not able to deal with things remotely, the team heads back as fast as we can, quite often with extra backup. As previously noted, we want things cleared up as much as the client does, and we take a very dim view of half-done work.

So, there you have it – a basic overview of the process from first contact to after care. While each case is unique, that's the basic pattern of events I'll be referring to as we make our way through the case studies that follow. I feel it's important that we start there because I want to make sure you understand what I'm going to tell you later. For me, one of the purposes of this book is to hold aside the curtain for a moment and let you see the wizard with his dials and switches. I don't think for a moment that you're going to look at me the same way you would a regular tradesman, because it's such a very different world, but I want you to see that we're people. We take a pride in what we do as much as anyone else. And we have families and messy break-ups and all the usual domestic rubbish that is part of modern life.

But then, so do the SAS.

Here are the two standard questionnaires sent to potential new clients at the beginning of the research phase of a case. They were developed as a means of giving us an overview and to help clients remember things that may have been forgotten. I've included them here to give you an idea of where we start – although things can go from here in many different ways, as you are about to discover.

Athanor Consulting Personal Crisis Questionnaire.

(NB Some of the questions here may cover information you have already told us. We apologise for the repetition, but it is important to have a written record of everything.)

Please answer all the questions in as much detail as possible. All information given will be kept strictly confidential.

Firstly, your full name, age, gender, marital status, address and telephone number.

How many people are living with you? Are they aware of your situation?

What religious affiliations or spiritual beliefs (if any) do you hold? How do these appear in your day-to-day life?

Are you or any of the residents suffering from any medical or psychological problems or have any history of such problems?

In as much detail as you can remember, please list the problems and incidents that you have faced. If you can remember dates, times and circumstances for these it will be very useful. Also note any actions you have taken in response to these incidents (anything from calling in psychologists or other medical advice to any other attempts to deal with paranormal forces, i.e. priestly exorcism). Also note who was present for each incident – and, as above, their ages, religious inclinations etc.

Have any of you had any involvement in the paranormal/occult before? (This could include 'dreams that came true', sensing when a person is going to telephone just before the phone rings, seeing ghosts, sensing unusual feelings from a person or place etc.)

Have you received any direct threats (physical or psychic)?

Do the phenomena seem to be based on your home or do they 'follow' you wherever you may be?

Athanor Consulting House Crisis Questionnaire.

(NB Some of the questions here may cover information you have already told us. We apologise for the repetition, but it is important to have a written record of everything.)

Please answer all the questions in as much detail as possible. All information given will be kept strictly confidential.

Firstly, your name, age, gender, marital status, number of children if any, address and telephone number.

How many people are living in the house and how old are they?

What religious affiliations (if any) do you, your partner and any other residents hold? (This includes whatever religious education your children have been exposed to.)

Have any of you had any involvement in the paranormal/occult before? (This could include 'dreams that came true', sensing when a person is going to telephone just before the phone rings, seeing ghosts, sensing unusual feelings from a person or place etc.)

Have any of you experienced any similar problems, or any incidents of a paranormal or unusual nature, before moving to the current property?

Are you or any of the residents suffering from any medical or psychological problems or have any history of such problems?

When you bought the house, was there any mention of problems from the previous tenants or the estate agent?

Have any neighbours mentioned problems (either with their own houses or rumours of problems with your property) that occurred prior to your arrival or with their own properties?

Has there been any publicity or news interest in the incidents?

In as much detail as you can remember, please list the problems and incidents that have occurred in the house. If you can remember dates, times and circumstances for these it will be very useful. Also note any actions you have taken in response to these incidents (anything from calling in plumbers or other workmen to any other attempts to deal with paranormal forces, i.e. priestly exorcism). Also note who was present for each incident – and, as above, their ages, religious inclinations etc.

Is there any possibility that someone is trying to force you to leave the house? Have you received any direct threats (physical or psychic)?

chapter three
MEET THE TEAM

As I've said before, not all phenomena are malicious. In fact, the sort of tales I've chosen for this book are the exception rather than the rule. If some kind of understanding can be reached, then blasts of psychic energy and running around shouting are pretty much unnecessary – which suits me because they're undignified and can play havoc with one's wardrobe (even if they are fun sometimes). To give an example of this, and to start the stories on a relatively up-beat note, I asked four of my colleagues to relate an example from their own experiences. Athanor is very much a team effort and our variety of individual backgrounds is what, for me at least, makes it such a pleasure to be part of. I've included a slightly humorous one of my own at the end, since my own experiences haven't all been as bad as the ones that come later.

To begin, here's an account by Jane Waterman that relates to dealing both with the dead, and the results of badly-performed magic. Jane is a respectable married lady with three grown-up children and a mindset rooted very firmly in the practical. She's also our first choice for relating to clients on site, as she combines strong skills as a back-up with an excellent ability to communicate not only with the living, but also with less conventional beings.

Jane Waterman: My ancestry is partly Scots, partly respectable English yeoman stock, and partly almost every other blood in Europe and some from further afield; I was brought up in a very ordinary town in the south of England in a very ordinary middle-class way, always excepting an enormous quantity of books of many kinds ranging from collections of fairy-tales written by authors including Lawrence Housman and Dorothy Wordsworth to the works of Karl Marx in German, any of which I was encouraged to read if I wanted and was able to.

Nobody talked specifically about mystical matters in my hearing that I can recall, at least until I was in my teens, and certainly my father would have cast academic and scornful cold water on any airy-fairy stuff of that kind. He has a most logical and ordered mind, and dislikes theories that lack any possible proof to back them up. In anything related to religion of any kind, he is agnostic veering towards atheism, whereas my mother, whose father was a rector, had a quiet and somewhat Quaker-influenced faith, although she never made any particular point of encouraging her children towards a belief in God.

Ever since I was quite a small child, certainly before I went to school, I have known that there were things that some people could perceive and others couldn't, just as there are ideas that some people understand and others don't. I don't recall that it ever bothered me: when one is very small, everything is slightly mysterious, and that doesn't matter anything like as much as such things as having the proper sock of a pair identical to the adult eye on the proper foot. I knew in a very vague way that some people claimed they saw 'ghosts' and that some people were afraid of them, yet the C. of E. primary school I went to a little later seemed entirely to approve of at least one ghost, they called it 'The Holy Ghost' and nobody was expected to be afraid of it, or him. Grown-ups had funny, arbitrary ideas all the time; this was just another grown-up strangeness.

I knew too that there was one bit of the Downs, in the Fair Mile up above Goring-and-Streatley, where our dog absolutely hated to go, and would even refuse to go sometimes, and where I always felt unhappy – I didn't find out until years later that this was a place where there had been a gibbet. I avoided it just as I would have done a manure heap on a pig-farm and it had about as much importance to me as that would have had.

My mother occasionally talked about the 'atmosphere' of a house being unpleasant, and sometimes she meant that the people in it were nasty or were always quarrelling, and sometimes I knew that couldn't be what she meant because the people who lived there were fine and never quarrelled at all. Later, in my early teens, I found out that she was sometimes very sensitive to things other people didn't notice at all and had been aware of at least two actual ghosts. One was a person who had committed suicide in a house her family rented for a holiday when she was fifteen and whose presence in the house made it impossible for two of the children on that holiday to sleep in that house, while the other four of the party were entirely oblivious to the grue. The other was a Mexican Indian from a very long time before, who came and inspected her and apparently approved of her when she first visited her Mexican sister-in-law. That Mexican Indian had driven some people out of the house by concentrated malevolence, but also had a very good relationship with one of my cousins, who talked with him about his life and got answers that made sense, when she was far too young to have known the history of the house or of the area. This seemed perfectly reasonable to me: why shouldn't someone who happened to be dead like some people and dislike others, just the same as people who were still alive did?

In other words I grew up with a personal awareness of what has been called 'the paranormal' or 'psychic phenomena' or what-have-you, and never thought twice about it in any wider way. It was all just another part of life, some good, some bad, nothing worth worrying about unless it had a bad effect on something I was doing or gave me nightmares like the book of Goya's pictures of the horrors of war.

As I reached my later teens I remained vaguely aware of psychic matters and mildly interested in them, and I found that readings I did with a Tarot deck (these were just coming back into vogue at that time and becoming available, and one of my cousins had written a book about them, which sparked my interest) were often surprisingly accurate, but so much else was so much more interesting that the whole matter got shelved for about ten years and it wasn't until some little while after I had married and left home that I had any particular reason to think about it again.

The first flat that my husband and I bought, as opposed to renting, was the top-floor flat of a Georgian terrace, with very low ceilings and small windows behind a parapet, and a flight of stairs inside the flat, behind our front door which opened onto the main stairwell. At the top of our private stairs was a hall with a small storage room opening off it to the left of the stairway, a bathroom to the right, and straight ahead of the top of the stairs the door of a bedroom to the left and to the right the door that led into the kitchen, beyond which were the sitting-room and the main bedroom at the far end of the flat. We lived there with a very sensible dalmatian dog (as sensible as a dalmatian ever is, anyway).

One week my husband had to be away for his work and I was left alone with the dog for the first time since we had moved in about six months before. On the first evening, I went to bed at about half-past eleven, and woke in the early hours needing to use the loo. I didn't bother to turn on the lights and went through the kitchen where the dog was sleeping in the dark. As I was sitting in the bathroom, I quite clearly saw, in the light from the skylight in the hall, a person moving quickly from the direction of the spare bedroom towards the head of the stairs. Being either brave or stupid, depending on your point of view, I seized the nearest weapon to hand (which happened to be a loofah) and leapt out into the hall shouting, 'Oy, you!' or something of the kind. There was nobody there.

I was slightly shaken, but decided I must have imagined it, particularly since the dog hadn't stirred in his basket in the kitchen until after I had shouted and he was generally an excellent and very noisy watch-dog.

I went to bed at about the same time on the next night and woke just before one o'clock and realised that the hall light was on. That upset me rather. I remembered then that on several occasions my husband and I had had arguments about who had left the hall light on last thing and wasted electricity, and this time it couldn't possibly have been him. I decided not to get up and go out through the kitchen to turn it off.

The following day I happened to meet a friend of mine who had an interest in psychic phenomena and mentioned the two incidents to him and he said that he and his wife would come round that evening and visit me, partly so that I shouldn't be left alone in a flat where I was now slightly nervous, partly because he very much hoped that if there was anything strange going on they might see it too. They duly came round and we checked the hall light and where its wiring went and made quite sure that only two switches, one just inside the front door and the other at the head of the stairs, had any effect on it. Then we sat in the kitchen talking until after midnight, leaving the hall light turned off. None of us noticed it turn on, but at about a quarter past midnight we noticed that it *was* on and both my friends got rather excited.

We went out into the hall, and my friend tried to 'get in touch' with any spirit who might be there, without success. Then we went and sat in the kitchen again, because it was more comfortable, and started talking about what might be going on, and quite suddenly, in the middle of nothing in particular, I found myself talking in a voice not at all like my own, higher and with a soft, West of England accent, about being a maid in the house. My friend was extremely surprised too, but he and his wife started to ask careful questions, which I found I could answer.

The girl, whose name was Dorothea, had been a maid in the house during World War One and had slept in the room that was now our spare bedroom. Among her duties (about which we got a lot of information we weren't particularly interested in!) she was expected to get up three or four times during each night to help either a nurse or a housekeeper, we couldn't quite get clear which, who was nursing the daughter of the house through what sounded like some sort of rheumatic fever; the invalid, a young woman in her early twenties, needed to be turned in her bed at night, and this needed two people. One night, the housekeeper/nurse had called up to wake Dorothea to come and help her and in her haste Dorothea had failed to pull her shawl round her properly, tripped on the trailing end of it, and fallen down the stairwell.

We concluded that she had been killed in the fall.

She kept on saying (or I kept on saying, but actually I was listening far more than I was speaking, from my point of view) that she must get downstairs to help with 'the young mistress', and seemed very unhappy at being somehow, she didn't understand why, delayed in doing her duty.

Eventually, my friend managed to make contact with her in the other direction and told her that it was no longer 1916, that it was time for her to move on and that the people she knew would all be waiting for her. She accepted this after some confusion and went away. The light in the hall never turned itself on again and I never saw her again and that was that. I would probably have put the whole thing down to over-active imagination on all our parts if it were not that during that night in the course of her ramblings about her life she had told us a lot about the communal garden of the terrace, including the positions of trees that were now of course long gone. At a later time I met a lady whose husband had been the gardener there for some while, and who had a plan her husband had made of the garden as it had been when he first worked there. The plan matched Dorothea's description remarkably, and there was no possible way that I could have known where trees that had been removed before I was born might have been. This did seem to confirm that somebody apart from the three living people and a dog had been present that night.

The thing that most struck me in the whole business, in fact, was that I was only afraid of this 'manifestation' because I didn't know what it was; as soon as I knew, I was no longer afraid, and it did me no harm whatever even when I *was* afraid of it. The ghost was the one needing help, really, not I. She wasn't hostile or sinister, just confused and a bit lost.

Later in that same year I was involved with another 'manifestation', this time in a flat into which a young couple who were friends of mine had moved and in which they seemed to have nothing but bad luck: from small things this had worked up to their dog, which had always disliked one of the rooms particularly, running out of the flat apparently in a panic as the front door was opened and being killed by a car in the road, and the wife breaking her baby's arm while putting a vest on the poor child. The people investigating this run of bad luck decided that the problem lay not with the ghost of an individual, but with what they called an 'artificial elemental', something that had built up over a period during which a living person or living people had behaved in a particular, and in this case, nasty way on the premises and had left a residue of emotions and behaviour lingering there.

The problem seemed to stem from someone living in the flat in the 1960s who had played with black magic in a half-baked sort of way, and left all sorts of unpleasant feelings lingering behind – what one of the investigators termed, 'leaving power-sockets switched on all over the flat' waiting for anyone sensitive to such things to get a shock from them. It was found that I seemed to be very good at locating these 'power-sockets', which could then be 'turned off' by other people who knew what they were doing – which I did not! I was simply a useful canary, as they told me; I said 'Tweet!' and pointed to places that made me feel uncomfortable. I'm glad to say that after almost a full day of rather unpleasant sensations for me, we seemed to have succeeded in making the flat a much better place to live in, and the young couple's bad luck ceased.

Again, one could hardly blame the 'ghost', which wasn't even sentient itself and had no will in the matter. I concluded that ghosts aren't necessarily evil or wicked.

Shortly after this I became pregnant and for the time being lost interest in everything except the new baby and the inevitable move into a house (flats with more than eighty stairs up to them don't mix well with a pram!). I next paid any attention to the paranormal when the baby was about a month old. I foolishly tried to catch a falling saucepan, missed, and poured boiling fat over my right hand and the kitchen floor. With a small baby I simply didn't have *time* to have only one hand I could use and, quite without thinking, as I plunged my hand into the cold water in the washing-up bowl in the sink, I said aloud, 'No! I haven't time for this! I simply *will not* be burned!' with absolute determination. Then I watched in fascination as the red, painful hand swelled briefly and then subsided again, within the space of about ten minutes, leaving hardly a trace of injury. I had never considered myself as a potential healer, but this alarmed me slightly: I was fairly sure that if I had power of this sort I ought to make certain that it was coming from the right source. I had an Evangelical Christian friend who had been thrown out of his church for healing a migraine for somebody without his action being sanctioned by the vicar – something, I may say, which I regarded as possibly the most appalling example of unchristian behaviour I had ever personally encountered, and I was shocked that the vicar had behaved so badly and allowed his 'elders' to be so unpleasant on such tenuous grounds. Even so, their determination that unsanctioned healing must come from Satan, however stupid I thought it must be, rattled me and I took myself to the nearest church I felt comfortable in and made contact with the vicar there. With my husband's entire approval I arranged for the baptism of my baby and myself – my mother didn't have me baptised as an infant because she was having one of her periodic vicarage-childhood-inspired rows with her bishop at the time I was born and she was refusing to have anything to do with him or his 'wretched church'. I felt that I would like to be sure that, if I did any healing, I was doing it as a member of a congregation and with approval from a direction I knew to be a good one: I might not be entirely sure which side I was on, at that point, but I knew which side I *didn't* want to be on. I did explain this to the priest and he was amused and pleased and gave me his permission to heal anyone I felt I was able to without going through the formality of ringing him up each time! He was a good man.

During the next twelve years or so I had occasion to heal some migraines, bruises, burns and fingers that had been crushed in doors. It seemed to work and I felt that it was a good thing to do. My eldest child too showed some healing ability; when he was about two he fell against a sharp concrete edge and cut his forehead open to the bone, a wound that required five stitches, and which, after the first horrific half-minute, didn't bleed at all (unheard-of for a scalp-wound) until the precise moment that the anaesthetic was injected. At this point he bled like a stuck pig until I told him firmly to 'think healing', when it stopped again – and the nurse retreated three or four paces looking terrified! He was able to heal himself when I encouraged him to do so, and sometimes extended his skill to small friends with cut knees, but gradually after he went to school he stopped doing it.

In my mid-thirties I met a woman whom I came to love and admire very deeply and who had a desperately painful condition of the spine that was gradually making it impossible for her to walk; this was believed to be arthritis, and not curable by conventional medicine. Because she was (and is!) a genuinely wonderful person, I made a real effort for her, visiting her every day for more than six months with my third baby, her god-daughter, in attendance and spending as long as an hour on each visit trying to make her back stop not just hurting but being wrong at all. I didn't succeed entirely, which isn't surprising when I learnt later that she not only had a severe problem with calcification of the bones of her spinal column so that it was pressing in on her spinal cord (eventually this needed a ten-hour operation to correct it), but also had an undiagnosed broken bone in her neck as the result of a car accident some years earlier. But for about a year I did help her to be able to walk and go about her life reasonably normally. This gave me a great deal more confidence in healing and forced me to believe that it really could work. I had been decidedly sceptical, if not of healing, of my own ability, which I felt was inferior to my son's.

I never tried to avoid these things, but for the first forty years of my life I never actively sought out anything in the way of psychic doings at a personal level. I was interested in the subject and visited stone circles and other ancient sites in a spirit of enquiry but without any particular purpose. It was interesting, for instance, to find out that when my son told me at Stonehenge, 'That stone is good for sleeping', he was quite right: there is a stone there which, if one leans against it, sends one to sleep almost instantly. One particular stone circle very much likes to have a small stone from elsewhere in the country brought inside it and left there. Another circle hated everyone for years because it had been abused by a group of people who enjoyed 'sacrificing' black chickens in it for no particular reason except their own general nastiness, and it had quite reasonably taken against humanity and started to try to cause road-accidents in its vicinity. But it all seemed fairly pointless, and without any particular application to everyday life and bringing up three children. Most of the things that people seemed to find terrifically exciting, like reincarnation (why were so many of them ex-Albigensians or Pharaohs, I always wondered), seemed to me to be entirely futile and without any bearing on my ordinary life.

Then in my forties I encountered the man who later founded Athanor, or rather re-encountered him after not having seen him for some years, and he invited me to help him in dealing with I now forget what small psychic problem a friend of his had been having, which I was happy to do. Over a few years, we seemed to come across more than our fair share of psychic problems and a group of people gradually began to gather who were both happy and able to help to sort them out.

In the end, it was decided that we could possibly reach more people with problems and do more good if we advertised and made our existence known, rather than relying on chance to bring people in trouble to our doors, and that is what was done. Charging money for our help was and is a necessary way to remain solvent ourselves: we simply can't afford to travel all over the country at our own expense, 'trouble-shooting' for people who may not even have a genuine problem and, by charging for our services, we may also keep away people who are not in real need of help.

Perhaps I have been lucky: I've never yet been hurt by a psychic manifestation. Frightened and made unhappy, certainly, but no 'ghost' I have encountered yet has been able actually to cause me physical damage. Until one does, I shall probably go on assuming that ghosts are more likely to be confused and unhappy than malign, and that if one can work out what their problem is and help them solve it, they will be quite glad to go away and make no more trouble for the living. After all, they don't really belong here and, once they become aware of it, they are generally quite willing to go away. Just as simple as that.

People being malicious is a different matter. On a few occasions I have come up against nasty happenings that are a result of conscious ill-wishing by a living person. In those cases I don't have the power to throw whatever it may be back into the face of the sender, so I'm glad to know one or two people who can. I don't really feel a need to heal someone who is so damaged spiritually as to be deliberately hurting another person, even if I were able to. I simply want him or her stopped, as quickly as possible, and if possible prevented from ever doing it again.

On that basis, I am happy to work with an organisation whose first reaction to a troubled situation is not to go into it with bell, book and candle to 'exorcise' at all costs – something I am sure must be needlessly unpleasant for ghosts! I prefer a more reasoned and less confrontational approach, first trying to find out what exactly it is that needs to be dealt with and then if possible using calm persuasion, only resorting to more ferocious tactics if it becomes clear they are absolutely necessary. It seems to me that this is just another, more widely-applicable aspect of healing, and healing is what I feel to be the most important part of any psychic's (and of any person's) business in life.

*

Next we move to Roger's account of how he ended up dealing with things like this and how he came to Athanor. Roger is in his thirties and assists mainly at long range, especially with remote viewing and sensing, and is our technical guru as well as providing an essential voice of scepticism when it comes to analysing information. He's also an excellent healer.

Roger: I was brought up as a rationalist Christian: there might be occasional miracles (more commonly long ago and far away), but one should not expect them in one's own life and anyone claiming any sort of magical or supernatural power was a fraud. Accordingly, when I realised that I could reliably spot people who would be unfriends or untrustworthy on my first meeting with them no matter how pleasant they were being, I assumed that everyone could do this but for some reason didn't; when this was disproved, I assumed it was simply a gift for reading body-language or something similar. Various school-friends messed around with Tarot decks and such like, but I never encountered anything that didn't have an obvious mundane explanation.

This continued until I became seriously ill with brucellosis at about the age of 16. For some years I was sleeping for extended periods and spending much of my waking time in severe muscle pain, unable even to read. For obvious reasons, I spent a fair amount of time in my own mind, prodding things to see what would change. One of the long-term results of this was that I became more open to evidence of unconventional events. When a friend was suffering from a severe asthmatic attack until the exact moment when I 'thought' about the reopening of his bronchioles, I did not automatically dismiss his sudden relief as a coincidence or a psychosomatic effect.

After I got better, I paid more attention to that sort of thing. I started to notice that my perceptions of people were significantly sharper than they had been; some people whom I'd previously have rated as 'untrustworthy' now felt actively rotten, like an old tree-stump full of worms. Increasingly, I got the sense that there was a great deal of magical nastiness in the world, both conscious and otherwise, and that I had the metaphysical equivalent of a sign over my head saying 'free lunch'. I eventually appealed to a friend whom I believed to take an interest in such things and was taught some basic shielding techniques. Some of them worked for me, others didn't, and I started to build on what seemed to suit me best.

I found that I could relieve pain, and often its underlying causes, in other people with fair reliability. I was given a set of Tarot cards that felt right to me in a way that no others had and had a fair level of success using them as a psychological tool. Once my perceptions settled down and became reliable, I started to become aware of what I can best describe as knots of unpleasantness; it seems that, given a suitable seed-crystal, negative feelings will coalesce and increase in strength. The result of this on a practical level is random mundane nastiness: a section of motorway where people drive much more closely to the person in front than they do elsewhere, a house in which people don't enjoy themselves and which they leave as quickly as possible, an electrical system that keeps blowing fuses even though there's nothing wrong with the supply current and the house has just been completely re-wired.

It appeared to me that, since I seemed to be unusual in being able to spot the knots that often form the centre of this sort of problem, it probably fell to me to do something about them. I am fundamentally an empiricist. If a technique works, I use it and improve it; if it doesn't, I discard it. I have read very little about magic as it is practised by other people and, if put in a traditional ritual setting, I find it extremely hard to take with any seriousness; it seems to me that a great deal of modern magical style has been influenced by Crowley's self-aggrandisement and a general wish for power even by genuinely talented people. I don't chant or wear a pointy hat but I do seem to be able to produce a practical and measurable effect that can be detected not only by other practitioners but by people with no belief in magic at all.

The friend who introduced me to shielding techniques later pointed out that I could be useful to a group that was trying to reduce Bad Stuff, more or less as I was already doing, and I have on several occasions worked with Athanor Consulting. Generally, I supply backup from a distance, particularly with map sensing, or cover the outside of a site against leakage in either direction while the remainder of the team works up close. I also continue to track and unravel knots of unpleasantness, which seem to be responsible for a wide range of apparently mundane problems – at least, the problems seem to go away once the knots have been undone.

One notable occasion was a case in which Athanor was working to treat a woman who had been diagnosed with a large cancerous tumour with a high probability of metastasis. I was able to work on her prior to the surgery (and during it, from a distance) along with the other Athanor team members. The medical team were somewhat surprised when a second biopsy showed that the tumour – which turned out to weigh about ten pounds – was benign and that no metastases had established themselves anywhere else in her body.

*

Now Daniel. Educated to PhD level, Daniel is our primary researcher, linguist and expert on Far Eastern culture. He speaks a number of languages fluently (including three dialects of Chinese) and has worked as an interpreter and language teacher. His background is primarily centred on the more esoteric disciplines of Buddhism, but that hasn't stopped him from working with a number of other western magical forms. His account, while complex, is a fascinating view of what happens when something doesn't necessarily speak the same language we do.

Daniel: I was doing some research for David just before this happened. He was working on a case in a small village out in the country. This place had its roots way back in the Doomsday Book, so there was some seriously old stuff around. A couple of days after they did the business, I had a very vivid dream. I saw a chart in the dream. It looked a bit like a Ouija board. There were all the usual alphabet letters on the chart. There were also some strange medieval characters too, as well as figures from the old Anglo-Saxon language. In the dream, I understood that I had to take a message from a dead soul.

When I get very lucid dreams like this, it usually means one thing. It means that something is really trying to get through. If there was a message for me from some outside entity then I had to use this chart to receive it. Right, so first of all I had to take the correct precautions. If you are going to start monkeying about with dead souls and their spirit messages, you had better make sure you have got a good psychic shield up. The shield acts as a filter. If you invite spirits into your head without a strong screen-door in between you and them, you risk getting well and truly possessed. Believe me, that is something you do not want. So I got that sorted out straight away. Then I set to work.

I drew a semi-circle of letters, just like I had seen in the dream. I grouped some of the letters together. I was going to use a pendulum to pick out the letters I wanted. If the gaps between them were too narrow, I would never be able to tell which one the pendulum was pointing to. So I put some letters into pairs. 'B' and 'P' went into the same box. I knew that medieval Runemasters did not distinguish between 'D' and 'T', so they went into the same box too. So did 'S' and 'Z'. Then I made some spaces for our 'lost' letters. In the Middle Ages, writing was all mixed up. They had Roman alphabet letters, like the ones we use today, but they also had the Runes and they jumbled them all up together. This meant that Old English had some extra characters to deal with. They called these letters 'ash', 'eth', 'thorn', 'wen' and 'yogh'. We use groups of letters like 'th' and 'gh' for these sounds now, but a dead soul from medieval times would expect to see plenty of these Runes on the chart, so they had to be there. I made one mistake, though. I lumped in the letter 'wen' (like our letter 'w') with 'F' and 'V'. Old English could not tell 'F' and 'V' apart, but the letter 'wen' certainly had its own identity. That was going to be important later. Then I made another box on the chart for any other 'odd' letters, like 'ö' and 'ø', just in case we were dealing with something that spoke some quite other language entirely.

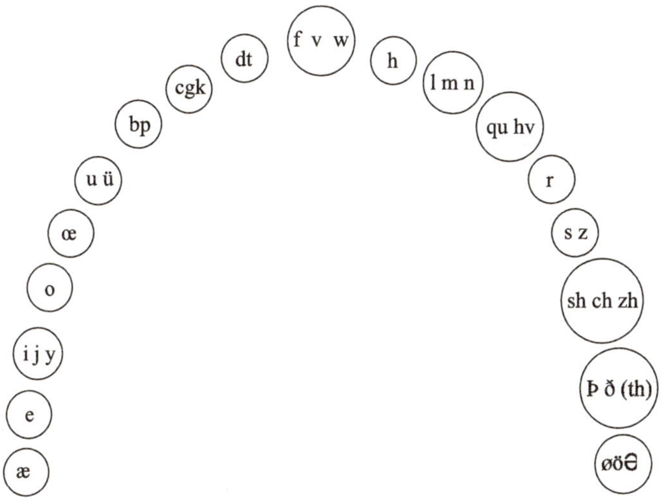

For all my experience with the pendulum, I had not really done this sort of thing before. That is, I had not tried to communicate with an external, and possibly dead, soul. I expected to find a few rational words in the message, but I was sure they would be mixed up with a pack of gobbledegook too. This is what normally happens with the Ouija board, after all. I held the pendulum with my right hand and wrote with my left hand. This is what I got:

ok tesfhœjþk? þk? el þe b þe b fesh þe b qum fœik

It didn't look very meaningful, but at least it did look like a sentence. Or perhaps two questions. The pendulum had, twice, turned round and round in a circle without pointing to any letter at all. I wrote this down as a question mark, because I didn't know what it was. But as I looked at the 'message', I realised that it was really meant to be a question mark.

That word with an 'fh' in it could not be right. I told you I should have kept the letters 'F' and 'wen' in separate boxes. That was certainly meant to be a 'wh', not an 'fh'. That told me that this language would have to be very late Anglo-Saxon, even early Middle English. In Anglo-Saxon they used to spell our 'wh-' words with 'hw-' instead. That put it somewhere around 1150 AD.

You see, because the dream had featured medieval letters, I had been expecting something in Anglo-Saxon, Middle English or Old Norse. I was pretty familiar with these languages from my old college days, but I never imagined I would have a practical use for them. Yet here I was, trying to communicate with a figure from those ancient times. If I was going to understand him, I would have to use my former skills all right, but not as a hollow academic exercise. This time they would be detective tools in a real psychic investigation.

I knew that the Anglo-Saxons often got the letters 'o' and 'a' mixed up, so that the word 'ok' was certainly meant to be 'ac'. That meant the same as our word 'but'. Because 'o' and 'a' could get muddled by the Anglo-Saxons, I could see that this entity was reading my 'oe' as the letter 'ash'. 'Ash' used to be written as an 'a' and an 'e' joined together, so this seemed reasonable. They would have looked just the same to a medieval monk anyway and it was the monks who did the writing in those days. This gave us one clear word: 'whaey'. In modern spelling that would be 'why'.

The monks didn't have paper in the Middle Ages, either. They wrote on animal skins. These were expensive and that was why they cut words down and shortened them to save space. So that word 'thk' was an abbreviation. In full it would have been 'thec'. Anglo-Saxon again. It was a form of the word 'thee'. We would say 'you' today. I didn't recognise the word 'tes' at all at first, so I looked it up in an Anglo-Saxon dictionary. I was surprised to find it was an alternative version of the word 'this'. 'El', I could not identify, but it looked like 'hell' with the 'h' dropped! So, that was another word sorted out, maybe.

Now, for a while, I could not make any sense of that repeated phrase: 'the b, the b'. I put that aside for a moment and concentrated on the next bit. That word was clear enough: 'fetch'. I had put 'sh', 'zh' and 'ch' together in one box and this was most certainly meant to be 'ch'. In Middle English they spelled 'fetch' many ways but most often as 'fechche'. The next word was 'qum'. Well, that really gave the game away. No doubt about it, this was a medieval word. It was clearly the word 'queme'. In Modern English, that means 'please'.

It was the last bit of the message that really puzzled me. I could not identify any such word as 'foeik', even if that 'oe' was meant to be a substitute for 'ae'. It made no sense for a while. Then the penny dropped. It was not one word. It was two! I tried separating it. 'Fae ik', perhaps, or maybe 'faei ic'? Then it struck home. This made sense! It would have been pronounced 'fay itch' and they would have spelt it 'faege ic'. Now I knew what it was! It meant: 'I am doomed to die.' We still have the word 'fey', even if we don't use it much any more, or not in that sense at least. In medieval times it was a word for anyone who looked as if he was doomed or on the way out. A pale and delicate youth would be 'fey' if he was on his way to fight the Vikings. He wouldn't last long, in other words. Now I looked at that repeated phrase again. 'The b, the b'. Suddenly it leapt into life. I had put 'P' and 'B' together in one box, remember. But this was not a 'B'. It was a 'P'! It could only stand for one thing: 'preost'. In Modern English, 'priest'!

Now I could transcribe the 'message' again, in full this time:

> 'Oc tes! Why þec? þec? 'el! þe P! þe P! Fechche þe P, queme. Fæge ic.'

And I would translate it like this:

> 'But this! Why you? You? Hell! The priest! The priest! Fetch the priest, please! I'm dying.'

This was a shock. It really made sense. These were the dying words of a man calling for a priest. So much for the gobbledegook theory! As a 'message' it did seem very heartfelt and emotional. Why should it come to me, though? I figured it had some connection with the job that David had been doing at that medieval village the previous Monday. I doubted that I had picked up an echo of something once said by someone back in the Middle Ages in the part of London I lived in. That was at the bottom of a boggy and uninhabited marsh back then.

The next question was the most difficult. Why was it directed at me? Was I the 'thec' our man was bawling out for not being a priest? It seemed likely. If you were a dying, medieval Christian, wounded in battle, a pagan like me might be the last person you would want to see. All the same, England was a Catholic country in the Middle Ages, after all, and I was not sure a modern Catholic priest would be any too pleased to hear about what I had been doing, let alone lend a hand here.

So, what action I was supposed to take? I felt what was called for was freeing the spirit somehow. Perhaps I could use the same technique that I had employed with the unquiet souls of suicide victims.

I use my own special formula in cases like that. This time, though, I got my books out and tried to translate it into the same language our spirit had used. Whether it was right or not was not so important. All that mattered was whether it would be understood. Anglo-Saxon is a language you translate from, not into. It is dead, after all. But then so was our man. I pinched a little bit from the Old English poets like Caedmon, and then added a little fiddling around of my own. In the end, this is the fake 'Anglo-Saxon poem' that I recited as a prayer. I called it into the night, along with the incense and the flickering tea-lights in my sacred space in the back garden. It goes like this:

Nu ic bidde thin, gast; on Godes faethme,
thu thaet med agan folme, ealdorgedael forthferde,
gehierest thu, gast, this gerisenlic aerende
ic, thin boda, thaet the hlifiath ic bidde,
this arweorthe leothsong the bebeodan;
molde tobredan ond tintreglic eorth afaran,
beo tha awyrgednes brocen wurde,
beo thu fram molde ne gebregdede
beo thu freolic sy, faeder ure,
ece Dryhten, in tir gedeorf aernan.

What does it mean? Much the same as the prayer I usually use, really. Of course, I had tried to make it sound Old English. It was not the real thing, though. I put it together in an inspirational haze. I can hardly remember what I thought it was supposed to mean now. I think it goes something like this:

'Now I bid thee, ghost, by God's good grace, thou, who with thine own hand, from life's realm went forth, hearest thou, ghost, this proper errand, I bid you, hear this song of mercy, shake off this earth, and leave this world, may this curse be broken, might thou not be bound to the earth, be thou free, by our father, eternal Lord, in glory let it run.'

Did it work? Well, our angry ghost has been very quiet since, so I would guess it did. Here's hoping, anyway.

*

And finally Ian Vincent, the founder of Athanor Consulting and my boss. We've been friends now for the best part of fifteen years and we've seen each other through some interesting times. Since many of the tales I've told involve this end of his magical career, he's chosen to remember the day that theory became practice and tell of his first case, long before Athanor was even an idea.

Ian Vincent: They say that any overnight success takes years of practice – and that was certainly true for me. My first 'ghost-busting' encounter took place when I was nineteen years old – so it was roughly twelve years or so of practice to get there.

When I was seven, I saw my first ghost-like apparition. Not so unusual – except that I saw it through another kid's eyes telepathically, which is not so common. I had an inkling that I was a bit odd before then – intense precognitive dreams will do that to you. (Those dreams were always about trivia, just odd moments of normality that I would see through déjà-vu at a later date... I think the triviality of the moments convinced me of their reality far more than any huge presentiment of disaster ever could have.)

Naturally, all this led me to quite an interest in the occult – a hard thing for most kids to study before they reach double figures. Fortunately, I had an incredibly helpful local library in Swanscombe, Kent. I'd already read all the children's books by the age of nine, so they gave me adult tickets. When I was ten, I had free access to the closed shelves and could order pretty much any book I desired. I was practising meditation and looking deeply into psychology and altered states of consciousness (well, as much as a kid with absolutely no access to or interest in drugs could...) and the more I looked, the more sure I was that there was some underlying reality, something magical that pretty much everyone else missed and I could not avoid.

I just couldn't work out if this was a blessing or a curse.

So by the time I was in my late teens I had quite a broad theoretical education in the occult and had spent some time looking into myself and trying to understand something about what I found there. I'd already passed through Christianity pretty swiftly and had found nothing in the traditional world of faith that called to me as loudly as the idea of magic itself, the energies of the universe having some coherence and that the mind could interact with them. I had experimented with inducing 'out-of-body experiences' by various (legal) means and trying to reconcile my image of the world with how I felt and acted. But something was missing – that internal bundle of theory and hope hadn't really crossed much into the 'real' world.

So I was in this pub...

I had a few friends who shared some of my interests, though perhaps not in as deeply obsessive a manner! We talked a little about some of this stuff, but not extensively. We met weekly in a pub in Dartford to hang out. There were four of us, myself, another man and two women. None of us were dating – though there was occasional flirtation. One of the ladies excused herself to powder her nose – the other sat with us, complaining of a headache.

I looked at her… and there was this most odd sensation in my mind. It was not in words at all, it was some other order of understanding, a kind of inner realisation. Somehow that time, that place, those people, catalysed all those years of study and thought.

I guess I was looking at her strangely. She said, 'I've just got a headache, Ian.'

I pointed at her head and said, 'No, you haven't,' and clicked my fingers.

Then she looked at me even more strangely – her headache had totally gone at that instant. (Even now, I have absolutely no idea if I cured her headache, if she made it go away at the suggestion, if the whole thing was placebo or coincidence. I just know it happened.)

The other woman in the group returned from the loo. She was, as they say, white as a sheet. The other guy there said something like, 'You look like you've…'

'I did,' she said. 'I just saw a ghost.'

That inner knowing again…

'Show me.'

She led me to the ladies' toilet. Of course, this did pose something of a problem but fortunately it was a quiet night. The woman who'd originally seen the 'ghost', a man-shaped dark cloud in one corner of the toilet, couldn't go back in, so she waited outside the door with the others and I went in.

There it was, just as she'd said, like a column of grey dust, man-shaped, somewhat dispersed. Now, up until then I had always been a pretty scared kid and been through a lot of bullying and such. Even though there were waves of fierceness and anger coming off this thing, I felt absolutely no fear. What I felt was immense sadness, pity. A sense of aeons of loneliness.

I tried to speak to the entity in my head. What I got back was not so much words as a stream of images, impressions. The gist of them was that this had once been a guardian, someone who had given himself up for human sacrifice to become a permanent protector of some ancient sacred site. Of course, that site had been lost centuries before, a town had grown up on the site... and now a pub and a ladies' toilet. The ignominy of it almost made me cry.

'You don't have to stay any more,' I said to it, 'You've done your duty.'

The thought came back, 'But what can I do now?'

'Come with me,' I replied, 'We'll think of something.'

That presence and I got on pretty well. In a sense, he became my 'familiar', my first magical ally. He also taught me perhaps the most important lesson in compassion I have ever learned – that just because something is scary, it doesn't mean that they're not also scared. The others in the pub noticed the entity had gone once I showed them and they never really talked about it again. It was my first, but not my last, encounter with the way most people can totally forget an occult encounter if it doesn't fit their idea of the world.

Many, many years later, I had an Athanor client who needed long-term protection and monitoring and this entity, who I hadn't heard from for quite some time, popped up and offered his services. For him, it was like going home again. For me, it was a circle completed.

*

For myself, I thought I'd simply mention a brief occurrence. One night, a few years back, I was staying in a hotel in Birmingham. It was a nice hotel, and quite old, and after a long day I was ready for some sleep. Having set my usual shields and locked the door quite firmly I settled down, closed my eyes and drifted off as best I could – to be honest, I don't generally sleep well in hotels unless I've had a couple of drinks and that night I was sober.

In the middle of the night, I was woken by something moving in the room. I knew that no one was coming through the door without making enough noise to wake me, so my first concern was that someone had come in through the open window. I decided to play possum, keeping my eyes closed but listening carefully to make sure I knew where the intruder was. There was no sound at all, which meant they were pretty good at the burglary lark as far as I was concerned. I wasn't planning on letting their impressive prowess be rewarded with my luggage, however, and started to slowly get myself ready to bounce out of bed and apprehend them. Still no noise, not even breathing.

The next thing I knew, I could feel someone by the bed. No sound, but I *knew* they were there. Where things got mildly confusing was that it felt as if they were trying to get into bed with me! Random people breaking into my room and trying to share my bed are not a normal part of my life and the fact that whoever-it-was couldn't get past my shields gave me the final clue that this wasn't a burglar (or a secret admirer). I opened my eyes, looked into the darkness and said the magic words that have dispelled so many unwanted elements over the years: 'Fuck. Off.' It took the hint, and disappeared.

To this day I have no idea what it was, or why it wanted to get under the covers with me, but it just goes to show why people should bring tea when they try to wake me before I'm ready: I'm grumpy in the morning!

chapter four

POLTERGEISTS (OR MORE LIKELY NOT)

It's really very rare, in my experience, for objects to start moving of their own free will. It's almost as rare for me to see a non-physical entity move something and I'm not sure I've ever seen telekinesis that could do more than affect the way dice roll (which is more common than casino owners would like to think). The things we see in the movies are somewhat more dramatic than the things that happen in real life and that's exactly the same in my field. I have yet to see dry ice rolling across the floor, or a room suddenly infested with insects, or a small child turn her head through three hundred and sixty degrees. I've heard people using voices they had no right to be using and seen a complete physical change come over people as something else moved into their heads and took over, so I know that some of the stuff I've seen on the big screen happens, but I'm sorry – no, actually I'm very relieved – to be able to say that real life doesn't have the special effects budget you'll find in Hollywood.

But stuff does happen. I've seen things trying to move without apparent reason, and I've felt things trying to hit me (not too hard, happily) and I've certainly felt the temperature in a room alter dramatically in a way that doesn't agree with my basic understanding of the laws of physics.

What I want to talk about here is the different ways in which these phenomena seem to occur. There are three basic causes for the cases I tend to see: magical operation, haunting by an actual dead person, and what we at Athanor refer to as artificial elementals, or tulpas. Let's look at each in turn.

MAGICAL OPERATION

There are a number of reasons that a magical operation can leave a place suffering from strange phenomena. Apart from cursing people, which is covered in chapter five, places may also be cursed, either by accident or by deliberate action. A deliberate curse needs to be dealt with on two fronts, the symptoms need to be neutralised while the cause is discovered and removed. Sometimes these are done simultaneously, sometimes in one order, sometimes the other. As with everything else we do, circumstances cause us to modify our response and reliance on the same plan time after time can lead to trouble.

The other magical cause for these effects is, for want of a better phrase, sloppy workmanship. The boom in occult interest that has taken place in the West since the start of the New Age movement in the sixties has led to far more people than ever before being able to learn magic and sadly this means that almost anyone can get away with putting out a book on the subject. Some of these books are better than others when it comes to the actual nuts and bolts of *doing* magic and this has led to a wide variety in quality of practice. The most common error encountered by the amateur is a poorly-executed shutdown after the operation is complete, what is commonly known as 'Closing down the circle', since most magicians work within a protected circle that is established at the beginning before the actual magic is done. The circle is important because it acts as a protective barrier between the outside world and the energies being manipulated by the magician and prevents those energies from affecting the work area in ways other than that intended.

Think of an X-ray machine. Radiation is emitted in a particular direction to produce an image on the photographic plate while the machine is designed to prevent that radiation from escaping in any other direction and causing harmful effects on those using the equipment. It's the same with magic. When a magical operation is completed, whatever it might have been, the energies used are closed down and the circle collapsed to ensure that no leakage has taken place. When that's not done properly then those energies leak into the surrounding environment and can lead to problems. Mild cases of this can cause cold spots or a particular 'atmosphere' in a place – a room, a house or an outdoor area. As the amount of energy increases, more pronounced effects are seen, up to and including psychological problems caused by stress and the effects of a full-blown haunting or demonic (for want of a better term) infestation, either by tulpas, which we shall come to in a moment, or by other entities taking advantage of the situation.

Under these circumstances, it can be dangerous to use magic at all. The forces at work in the area can interfere with even a properly-constructed circle to cause unforeseen side-effects and possible harm to those involved, so a particular attention to detail is required when dealing with them. The two most effective strategies that I favour are either draining or earthing the energy in an area, much like a battery or electrical circuit, or to sterilise the area by bathing it in sufficient energy to interfere with what was already there to such an extent that it can no longer hold any form of coherence. Sometimes a mix of the two is required.

There is, of course, a simple way to prevent any of this from happening. Practical magic is dangerous and forgetting that is an easy way to find out just how dangerous it can be. While it is not my business to tell anyone what to study or how, experience has shown that anything less than hard work and absolute diligence with regard to safety in the magical arena leads to trouble. Too many people seem to be reading one book and thinking themselves an archmage, and it just doesn't work like that – any more than a couple of driving lessons qualify a person to race cars professionally. If beginners want to study and to try rituals and apply magic to their lives I couldn't be more delighted. We're an oppressed minority finding our way into the sunlight of a modern age where we can discuss these subjects openly and honestly without fear of persecution, arrest or worse for the first time in almost two thousand years. All I would ask is that those who practise take the time to understand what they're doing and why it's important and then be sure to do it properly. Doing one's best doesn't cut it here: it's either right, or it's wrong. If it goes wrong, then there might well be Hell to pay.

HAUNTING BY AN ACTUAL DEAD PERSON

This is rarer than most people think. On the whole, dead people are smart enough to get on with whatever comes next and not waste time hanging around trying to bother the living. When someone does decide to hang around, they either have some particularly pressing reason (some form of unfinished business, for example), an enormous emotional attachment to a place (frequently trauma-related), or they simply haven't realised that they're dead and are suffering from a rather extreme bout of confusion.

The confused ones are simplest to deal with, although simple doesn't necessarily equate with easy. In essence what one has to do is get the poor unfortunate to accept that they are in fact dead and need to move on and make room for the living. Simple enough in theory, but getting their attention can often be something of a challenge and there are times when they simply don't believe you. At this point it's down to powers of persuasion and making a convincing argument; magic isn't always just a matter of waving wands, after all. Once you've got them to understand the situation, however, it's relatively painless to get them to move on to wherever they're headed and the chances of any after-effects are pretty slim.

When it comes to unfinished business, things can get a little trickier. The first problem is to strike up enough of a dialogue for you to be able to find out what exactly the problem is and what needs to be done about it. If it's an older problem, then some historical research may be required to find out exactly what they're on about in the first place. Things get even more complex if a particular building or object isn't there any more, or if it's changed hands in the intervening time period. When something like that happens, we're often back to the diplomatic arts: the task can't be performed, and their only option is to write it off. This doesn't always work and can force one to take more aggressive removal measures if the ghost is causing trouble to the living.

In the case of emotional trauma, the possibilities open up considerably. When someone dies violently, for example, they can find themselves trapped at the site of the death or occasionally at another familiar place related to it. At times like this, they feel that they are unable to leave and need help to do so. This can be anything from a kind word and permission to leave to some form of minor ceremony that sends them on their way – a second funeral, if you will. Opposition is unlikely, since they're generally grateful for the chance to get on with things and happy to be on their way.

The more challenging cases come when the person doesn't want to go. Either they insist on the completion of a now-impossible task, or they have an agenda and don't appreciate the interference. The most disturbing of these situations is when the entity in question deliberately means harm to those in the area and that's when measures have to be taken swiftly. A full exorcism can be a dangerous thing to do, which is why not many people are qualified to do it even within the formally established religions. It can also be traumatic to all concerned, not least the dead person on the receiving end, and thus is a measure of last resort. However, when it comes to the safety of the living versus the feelings of the dead, there's no contest: the living matter, and the dead guy's on his way.

There have been cases where a dead person with a history of violent behaviour has attempted to continue their proclivities in death. This is where things come closest to the movies, both in the risk presented to those living in the area where the criminal is based, and the measures that can be required to remove it. There will be attempts to disrupt the proceedings and there is a real risk that if the spirit is capable of telekinetic activity there will be some kind of physical violence. For this reason, it is imperative to clear the working area of all non-essential personnel and ensure that everyone knows exactly what is to be done before the work begins.

Overall, this is an extremely hazardous thing to do and it is a credit to most professional mediums that they know better than to try anything more than the persuasion method.

Exorcism is an extremely specialised task that calls for a great deal of training, a very particular skill set, a confidence in one's abilities that borders on arrogance and a team of people who work well together under pressure. It's really not something to try if you have any choice in the matter.

As I have stated previously, this book is not a 'how-to' sort of manual and I shall leave describing the full process of such matters to those better able to instruct than myself. I personally recommend leaving things like this to experts.

ARTIFICIAL ELEMENTALS OR TULPAS

These are entities created from concentrations of psychic energy. They can either be created specifically by a magician to perform a particular task, or can occur spontaneously in areas that have high levels of psychic energy as the result of a strong emotional release. They are by far the most common entity we encounter at Athanor and as such we have fairly well-established ways of dealing with them. We generally find that the spontaneous variety causes the most trouble, since it finds itself suddenly created with nothing to do. As in a small child, boredom leads to mischief, and people can find themselves suffering from strange occurrences as the tulpa tries to either define a purpose for itself or just looks for ways to amuse itself. Sometimes it can be more of a help than a hindrance if it decides to be useful to those living where it has come to be, but that is in atmospheres where people are happy and generally well-adjusted. Unfortunately, the intense release of emotion that helps bring them about is most often linked to negative emotions and that gives them an unhappy disposition from the start. This brings about a situation where they actively seek to cause more misery in a desire for sustenance and growth.

Most situations that are brought to us as hauntings turn out to fall into this category, since the observed effects are very similar. There is an oppressive atmosphere, people catch glimpses of something at the corner of their eye, or things go missing and suddenly reappear in their original location. Sometimes this is also mistaken for fairy activity, but actual cases of the fey interacting with humans are now very rare indeed.

Since people aren't in the habit of calling us to remove benevolent activity, we deal exclusively with the less pleasant end of the spectrum. Once a tulpa has been identified as the cause of a problem, the task is to catch or corner it, and then eliminate it. Since these are artificially created entities, there is nowhere to which they can be returned and so they must be destroyed. This process generally involves draining them of energy to a point where they can no longer hold themselves together and then hitting them with a concentrated blast of energy to effectively blow them apart. The area is then cleared of any remaining energy using standard techniques and the job is done.

Tulpas (the word comes from Tibetan and means 'thought-forms') are also used as magical servitors, generally tasked with a particular purpose in mind and programmed to expire when that purpose has been completed. Unfortunately, as with circle-closing, not everyone who creates one does it quite as efficiently as one might hope and these then go on to look for something else to do. The procedure for dealing with these is basically the same, although some of them are more able to defend themselves if attacked. The basic forms of combat magic are normally enough to take care of their defences, however, and matters are normally brought to a close without any undue inconvenience.

OTHER CAUSES

One other phenomenon that is frequently mistaken for haunting is known in some circles as RSPK, which stands for Recurrent Spontaneous PsychoKinetic phenomena. We generally use the term to describe any phenomena where objects appear to move without cause, doors slam or similar effects are observed until another reason for these has been determined. RSPK is frequently referred to as poltergeist activity, but actual ghosts are fairly rare in my experience and we are not comfortable using the term unless we've come to the conclusion that is indeed the cause.

Many theories exist as to the causes of RSPK, including uncontrolled psychic activity – particularly in teenage girls. It is generally agreed among practitioners of the occult arts that any such act requires a great deal of energy to succeed and that guaranteed results are almost impossible. A number of governments, most notably the US and Russia, have sunk an awful lot of money into researching psychic phenomena over the last few decades, apparently without success in quantifying them. The most public example of this is the data retrieved from the US government's Project Stargate (which dealt specifically with applied uses of remote viewing in intelligence and military scenarios), which the CIA had analysed by Professor Jessica Utts (now Professor of Statistics at the University of California, Davis) and noted debunker Professor Ray Hyman of the University of Oregon. While Utts noted a statistically significant effect, Hyman concluded zero results. Going with the results that best fitted the political environment of the time, the CIA followed Hyman's recommendation to terminate the project in 1995.

Of course, there are also more prosaic causes – and we don't automatically discount them in the desire to find an esoteric reason for activity. Plumbing, damp, dry rot... there are any number of things that can cause spooky-seeming effects and they have to be eliminated before we decide that we're able to help with a problem. Generally, this is covered as part of the screening and analysis phase and we are able to recommend plumbers and suchlike with experience of working in areas that have had magical/psychic phenomena for the purposes of eliminating more mundane reasons for their trouble.

In any case, correctly identifying and understanding what is happening to the client is the first and probably most important phase of an assignment. It is the initial point that determines how everything else will proceed and what steps need to be taken to ensure the safety of both the client and the team. Of course, there are occasions where one thing appears to be another and we maintain a fairly high level of flexibility so that we can adapt to changes in the situation quickly and without fuss. As Napoleon Bonaparte once said, 'No battle plan ever survives first contact with the enemy' and, while we may have a good idea of how to proceed with a situation, it doesn't necessarily follow that whatever we're dealing with is going to cooperate with us.

chapter five

CURSES AND THEIR REMOVAL

What is a curse?

Put simply, a curse is a directed act of magic specifically designed to cause harm to another person. This is generally considered a bad thing and most certainly frowned upon in civilised magical groups. Sadly, not all magical groups are civilised and there are also some people out there who fire curses off without anyone else knowing. Finally, there are those who do it without even realising it themselves. These are people who need help and to be taught how to stop it. Everyone else who uses them is a bad guy... including me.

Because, gentle reader, I have slung more than the odd hex myself over the years. I like to think it's always been for the right reasons, but are we necessarily the best judges of our own morals? Who's to say, really? If it comes down to me throwing a curse, it's generally what we refer to as a 'counter-hex': something designed to remove an aggressor's ability to attack a client, or distract them while we seek an alternative solution. It's not something I particularly enjoy, but sometimes it's a necessary tool for what I do. If there is a Last Judgement at the end of the game, then I may be in a little trouble over this; we all know what passes for flagstones on the road to Hell.

Curses come in three basic categories: ones that mess with either the mind, the body, or the life of the target. They're less common than you think, but more common than I'd like to think. The general means of laying one is the same as for all magic: declaration of intention, focusing of will, calls for assistance where applicable, and delivery to the target. Methodologies vary depending on the system used to lay the curse, but they have enough in common for me to deal with them.

Let's look at the various types in more detail.

CURSES THAT MESS WITH THE MIND

Curses can cause psychological difficulty in a number of ways. A doctor will tell you that, if a patient believes themselves to be cursed, then any number of psychosomatic symptoms might be seen. A psychologist will tell you that irrational fears can affect the mental stability of a patient. A magician will tell you that, if you can mess with someone's head, then they're yours and you can do whatever you want.

I consider 'love spells' to fall under this category also. It's one thing to make changes in yourself to become more attractive to another, but if one decides to use magic to effect the feelings of another towards yourself, that's pretty naughty. Any use of force to over-ride another's will is bad and just because it can't be seen magic isn't immune from that value judgement.

When one chooses to attack the mind of an enemy, it is normally with a specific effect in mind: emotional instability, some kind of fixed mania or difficulty in holding ideas and concentration are most common. Once the curse is in place, it grows to cause changes in the target's perception. Here we encounter an amusing side-effect of modern culture: in a primitive society, a target will consider a curse as a viable possibility, see a specialist and have the curse removed quickly and efficiently. Here, in the supposedly more advanced societies, it's more likely than the target will provide any rationale they can before finally admitting the possibility of a non-physical directed cause. This frequently means that by the time I see a curse, it's firmly emplaced and the client has become used to it being there. This makes it a little harder to remove, but not impossible.

CURSES THAT MESS WITH THE BODY

This can be anything from insomnia to wasting away. The power to strike people and animals sick was traditionally one of the accusations levelled at witches during the hysteria of the seventeenth century and earlier. It's also more common as an unconscious attack than the other two, since when we wish to harm another we generally think in terms of injuring them physically: a punch or something similar rather than wanting to drive them nuts or cause their marriage to break up.

CURSES THAT MESS WITH THE LIFE OF THE TARGET

From 'I don't want him to get that promotion!' to 'I hope she leaves him so I can have her' to 'After what he did to me, I hope he loses everything!', curses that affect the life of a target are the most frequent self-misdiagnosis by potential clients. In fact, this is where we have to take the most care, because it's not always easy to distinguish between a run of bad luck and someone specifically trying to ruin your life. Most of the people who come to us believing they've been cursed are simply wrong. They're hoping for a quick fix, for someone to make it all better for them in an instant, for a reason to believe that it's not their fault.

Mostly, it's not a curse. In the same way that we attempt to eliminate all possible physical causes before working on a location, we try to examine the course of the client's recent history to see at which point a curse may have been placed. Generally, one can tell the difference after an interview, and frequently from the biographical questionnaire alone. I'm not trying to be deliberately harsh, but I can't fix everybody's life; some of the time I can barely keep my own under control. I can't give succour where I cannot help, any more than I'd want to give anyone else false hope. I'm not a psychologist either and sometimes all these people need is someone to talk to. I don't mean to sound as though I'm belittling the problems of others, because I certainly don't want to, but there are things I cannot do, and sitting down with someone to help them understand where they've made bad choices falls into that category.

That said, curses are becoming more common. The increased popularity of occult study has led to people trying magic 'just to see if it will work', or experimenting with curses or love spells because they don't quite understand the ramifications of their actions. Frequently, they have no idea of how to remove the curse when they see what they've done.

So what do we do about a curse, if that is indeed the problem?

We start with a really good look at the thing – trying to understand what it's doing there. As with everything I handle, the more information that can be gained, the better. I tend to see curses as puzzles, like a really complicated knot. The trick is to find a gap in the thing, like a loose end. From there, I can look at ways of taking it apart. Most competent magicians who use curses tend to leave them booby-trapped so that a simple 'fix-it' won't actually work. Not only that, I've seen a lot that let their casters know when someone's fiddling with them.

We had a case recently that ended up as a pitched fight between myself and the caster while Ian was actually doing the removal. Initially, I was in a passive role, soaking up and diverting what was being thrown to distract the process. While I was stopping most of it from getting through, there was enough to keep Ian busy trying to do two things at once. So we decided that it was better for me to take a more aggressive route. In any magical operation, there's a connection between the caster and the target. Many people forget that this goes both ways, so as the opposition was sending stuff down the link, it was there and available for me to hijack. It actually makes life more convenient, since one is spared the laborious task of tracking a target and establishing the connection. It's all laid out for you, and all that needs to be done is to hook into it and start the distraction. Once I'd started being antisocial back at him, the person responsible for the curse was too busy dealing with me to be able to harass Ian and the client, allowing Ian to actually get on with the job. Circumstances like this also allow us to make it very clear that any attempts to re-establish the curse will be met with reprisals. We know how to hit the caster and they know we know. Since a decade of taking these things apart has made me pretty good at understanding how curses are constructed and delivered, I have access to techniques that can get pretty unpleasant, including messing with a person's energy to the extent that they can't do magic any more – they just can't move enough energy the right way. It's a nasty thing to do to another magician, and I'd hate to have it done to me because magic is a very important part of my life. That said, if somebody's using their multi-tool to hurt people, you take it away.

Who am I to judge whether this is right or wrong? Good question. I'm a practical sort of chap and try to see it simply: if you're hurting people, I'm going to stop you. This also raises another question that we have to ask when somebody comes to us with a curse: why? What have they done to bring this about? Is this someone who got caught being naughty and ended up on the wrong end of someone like me, or are they an innocent victim? If they've been misbehaving and somebody stopped them, I'm not going to be particularly inclined to restore their ability to wreak havoc.

It's not always as easy to judge as we might hope. But we do our best to be careful. As with every other potential client, we question, we interview and we research. We've turned down cases because of moral ambiguity that made us uncomfortable and will continue to do so. When we take any kind of case, we're standing up to fight for the client, and we need to be sure that the client's worth it. It's never been just about the money.

There was a case where a woman came to us and asked for help. She knew for sure that it was a curse, because she'd cast it. She even told us what she'd done and how. Now she wanted to reduce the effects of the curse because it had gone too far and was affecting her as well as her ex-husband, who was the target. In fact, her ex was getting over it and the effects were starting to show up and get in the way of her life. We talked to her about it, trying to understand her motives both for the curse and its removal. She was unrepentant, she'd do it again as long as it didn't affect her and she still wished him ill. While I know all too well how painful a messy break-up can be, there was no way we were going to help her. We gave her instructions on how to end the whole thing, and sent her on her way. We weren't going to help her fine-tune an attack on somebody else just because their marriage was over.

Who are we to judge? Just people, same as you. But some things are just plain wrong.

Another enquiry came in from the United States. A man had bought a farm and, a year after moving in, his animals were dying. A little research found that the livestock there had been dying for years, that the groundwater wasn't exactly ideal and the earth itself in a less-than-ideal state. Unfortunately, the financial woes of farming are universal and he didn't have the money to move. He was desperate. Then he found out that part of his property was a Native American burial ground. Seriously. We had a moment while looking at the information where Ian and I looked at each other and confessed that, even though we knew it wasn't a case for us, we just wanted to go and see it. This sort of thing only happens in the movies, we thought, and the chance to actually go to a place like this was astoundingly tempting. There was, however, a better option: we found that the tribe in question was still very much in existence and suggested he talk with them. While it was something we might have been prepared to assist with if the tribe was extinct, having the right people attend to it was better for everyone. We also felt he might benefit from talking to a lawyer, since he obviously didn't have all the facts when he purchased his property.

We've also had clients who have been on the receiving end of campaigns of constant malign activity. One of our higher-profile clients spent a fairly long period of time putting up with all sorts of physical objects placed on their property, each triggering a malign effect when they were picked up. It took us an awful lot of time to deal with this: responding to each attack, defusing objects and putting together a profile of those responsible. It is an unfortunate effect of becoming publicly known for doing something well that some people take an irrational dislike to an individual and that seemed to be the case here. Because the attacker was careful to cover their tracks, it took time to understand what was behind this. We followed standard procedure, ensuring that the client had no unpleasant skeletons in the cupboard that could have led to the situation as it stood and, once we were satisfied about things, we were happy to go full throttle.

It took a fairly long time to track this down, as the place where the items were being left had a certain amount of traffic: mainly parents taking their children to and from the nearby school. Since the client hadn't noticed anyone in particular passing by regularly we surmised that one of these parents might have been responsible, dropping something as they passed. It was a waiting game: each time they tried something on they gave us a little more information. The client was still being affected by the attacks, though, so we had an amount of fire fighting to do there. But again, it was more information. Eventually, the attacker did the one thing we'd been hoping for: they screwed up. We were able to get enough of a psychic trace to give us enough information to plan a response. It seemed that one person had persuaded a group that our client was some kind of black magician who needed to be eliminated. This was why we'd had trouble pinning it down: there had been a number of people acting in concert, and because their hate wasn't particularly directed towards the client they hadn't left that much of a trace for us to work with: the stronger a feeling is associated with an object, the easier it is to trace. But now we had something with the instigator's own residue on it and that meant we could do something proactive at last.

Making a decision about what to do wasn't as simple as usual. The instigator had suckered what would have been an innocent group into doing their dirty work with pure motives. While we weren't going to go after the group for being foolish enough to believe the lies they'd been fed we did need to make sure that they understood it was time to stop. After some discussion, it was decided to make an example of the instigator in such a way that the group would know that further action would lead to further consequences. We were going to throw a curse of our own back.

I'm not going to go into the details for two reasons. Firstly, I've said before that this isn't a 'how to' book and, secondly, because even if it was there's no way I'd tell you how to deliberately harm someone else. It's morally ambiguous at best and at worst is going to end up with me doing some fairly major explaining at the gates of the next world. Suffice to say that three of us sat down to start work, and I gave the instigator a case of temporary insanity and a compulsion to confess all next time they saw the group. We never saw any more activity from that quarter, so I like to think the message got through. We then made a few extra arrangements to protect the client's home and the area around it, including the relocation of a protective spirit whose original home had been destroyed some time previously (see Ian's part of chapter three) and that we'd been looking for a way to help for some time. This seemed like a perfectly good way of taking care of both issues at once and has improved the local gardens at the same time.

Then there are love spells. The nastiest one I've seen was a few years back. A man was obviously attracted to a woman who was involved with someone else and had been subtly making his suit without getting anywhere for some time. Having built up a friendship with her, he persuaded her to go to a local ancient site with him to watch a sunrise. All fine so far, and to this point it had been a simple friendship. But while they were there, it seems that they read a poem together: one that had magical connotations, with a side order of 'together forever'. As far as we can tell, this was the kicker. What was particularly tragic in this instance was that because she'd said the words herself of her own volition, there was very little we could do about it. She was suddenly completely in love with her friend, and left her partner soon afterwards. The partner was a magician himself and could see that something was wrong, but had no idea of how to deal with it so he brought it to us. We did what we could to work at it from a distance, but since she was completely happy with the new arrangement, all we were able to do was let it take its course and accept that you can't win them all. That stung like a bitch, I can tell you.

Finally, we had another client who claimed that a famous musician was cursing her. When a client claims any kind of association with a celebrity, we make sure to run a check via our own means and in this case knew someone in the alleged attacker's social circle. It didn't take long to establish two details that had bearing on the case: that the client had indeed been associated with that musician some time previously and that while the alleged attacker had some interest in the occult at the time, they no longer had that interest in any meaningful way and certainly weren't practising. We ended up deciding not to take the case, on the grounds that we felt that no paranormal or magical attacks were taking place.

To close this chapter, and after some discussion with my colleagues, I have decided to share one piece of practical magic with you. This is the standard technique we teach our clients when some form of long-term personal shielding is required. Obviously, we can't be there all the time for them and it would be ridiculous (not to mention unethical) to expect anyone to keep us on a retainer where it was not necessary. I personally feel that this is something that everyone should know how to do and it's a technique I use when I'm travelling through London on the Tube to stop myself from being affected by the general unhappiness that seems to be felt by many of my fellow passengers. So despite my insistence that this is not a book of practical techniques, I present for your use the briefing we refer to as:

Shield 101

The first thing to understand about raising a psychic shield is that, like any kind of psychic action or magical act, it all starts with breath. It is not for nothing that in every society that has a word for magical energy, all those words are synonyms for breath.

So, start with being aware of your breath, how each inhalation fills your body with energy, how each exhalation pushes the stale air and energies from you. Realise that as long as you are still breathing, you can never run out of life's energy. Always breathe in as deeply as you can – try to feel the breath opening your diaphragm, filling your lungs from the bottom up.

Then, as you inhale, feel that energy fill you completely, nourishing the very core of your being. Some people feel this in their heart, others in their stomach or solar plexus – wherever you experience this, let that point be the centre which your shield will grow from. Hold the breath for a second.

As you exhale, picture your breath as moving not just from your lungs, but passing through your whole body. Feel it pass through you, out of every pore and opening, cleansing you as it moves through you. Especially feel it coming out of your feet, pushing into the ground. Also feel the energy rooting through your feet, literally grounding you, letting your energy touch the deeper energy of the Earth. (Some people feel a tingling or other body sensation doing this. It's just your energy talking to your body. Don't worry about it – embrace it. If it gets too much, push it out through your feet-roots into the earth.)

You might need to do this a few times before the flow of energy feels right and you become used to breathing in this conscious way. Take your time. To steal a phrase – feel the Force flow through you.

Once you are ready, use your next exhalation to push that energy out again, but this time shape it in your mind into a field of rainbow light covering your whole body. Surround yourself in this moving rainbow.

When you next inhale, imagine the air moving through this rainbow field, passing through the colours, each colour filtering a different negative aspect, leaving only pure air and energy to fill your lungs. Again, sense that the inhalation moves into you through your skin, from the soles of your feet to the top of your head. Feel the core of you filling... then breathe out again.

Practise until it is, literally, as easy as breathing.

As long as you breathe, even while you sleep, that rainbow shield is there, nourishing and protecting you. Sometimes you might feel that it needs a little more energy, so direct more breath into it. Try to let the feeling of its presence become a constant background sensation – with time you may be able to sense different aspects of it, be able to tell when it's working harder to protect you from something. Think of it as an extra layer of skin, just as alive and responsive to the outside. And, like your skin, it's there to protect you... always.

chapter six
WEIRDNESS IN THE WORKPLACE

I'm not going to talk about our corporate clients. With individuals, I can disguise their identities easily enough; that's what I'm going to do in all the cases that follow but one. But companies are different. While the corporate environment is one of sameness, the individual characteristics of a company are far more identifiable – especially if you've worked there. Since it's entirely possible that most employees won't have a clue that their company has employed somebody like me but would recognise an environment we've both worked in, I've decided to discuss this as a general subject with examples rather than talk about one case.

I became interested in what makes workplaces go bad when I entered the world of work. Some of the places I interviewed in were far less pleasant than others and the people inhabiting them correspondingly worse-looking. Sad to say the situation hasn't changed much over all, and I think that you might recognise some of things I mention here in your own place of employment.

Haunted offices are less common than haunted homes. People very rarely have the kind of attachment to their places of employment that would lock them into place. An exception here is older factories. In the days of the Industrial Revolution, health and safety weren't much regarded and people died, often in grisly accidents involving machines. While an office job might not cause enough emotion to keep the remains of a personality in place, being ripped to shreds, or crushed, or suffocated is a lot more likely to have that effect. Pubs quite often have things going on, too – and I've got a tale to tell there, but you'll have to wait for chapter twelve.

So what do we find in offices? Generally, it's a matter of dealing with negative energies. Most offices have a stock of that: people hate their job, their boss, their colleagues and their customers. They hate the necessity to work. They hate commuting. Be honest with yourself for a second: do you actually enjoy working? If you do, you're a rare creature. I generally enjoy what I do, but it leaves me tired, frustrated, angry and occasionally despairing about clients and the world in general. So, if that's someone who *likes* their job, imagine what kind of emotional roller coaster someone who doesn't is riding. Now stick them in an open-plan office with thirty or so other people. There's no privacy, no respite from the pressure. In some offices, the length of time you spend in the toilet is monitored to make sure you stay productive. The number of calls you take in an hour, or the number of keystrokes at your computer, or the number of shelves you fill, or whatever it is you do, someone's watching, making you work harder, keeping the pressure up. For all their much-vaunted training, managers are not always good communicators. Self-expression is discouraged – wear the correct dress or be sent home.

I'm not saying that it's wrong for a company to want to get value for money from its employees. But there are ways of doing it that turn offices into nothing more than battery farms and there are ways that treat employees like people. The former approach is generally the cause of difficulties, poor staff retention and a general air of gloom over the whole workforce. This spreads from employee to employee as each drags the other's mood down.

I've seen entire open-plan offices of fifty to a hundred people where nobody smiled. Sure, the managers were allowed a few personal effects on their desks, but employees sat at a desk with a phone, and a computer and whatever they needed to do their jobs; nothing else was allowed because the company enforced a 'Clear Desk' policy. Nothing personal, unless you're a manager. Side screens divided each employee from their neighbour, and conversation was discouraged. Of course, the managers were expected to enforce an atmosphere of jollity and *esprit de corps* that just wasn't there because people couldn't bond. So the atmosphere of the place was depressing and wasn't helped because almost all the staff were temps with no job security or feelings of loyalty to the company. People were arbitrarily dismissed with no need for notice, because they had no contract and, while the temp agencies responsible for staffing this battery farm had an office on site, there was a distinct impression from some of the liaison personnel that the staff were just replaceable commodities not worth getting to know.

The other parts of the company employed people properly and treated them far better. These parts were more profitable, had better retention rates and happier people. But the first office seemed to end up going through the entire available workforce of its town and it got to a point where they couldn't hire enough people to keep up with the losses caused by attrition and the summary justice within. The solution was classic corporate thinking: they opened an office in a new town, and expected some of their more loyal temps to travel two hours each way to teach the new office how to do the job.

The simple fact is that misery loves company. If you take

an approach that makes people miserable, then that misery will build upon itself and spread throughout the working environment. This applies in the home as well, but is more likely to happen in an office because many people resent having to go to work at all. I've noticed that companies who spend time and trouble to create a decent environment for their employees have less sickness, absenteeism ('throwing a sickie' being different from actually being ill) and attrition than companies who are perceived not to care. Something as simple as taking a genuine interest in your staff can make the difference between people who are happy to work for you and people who would rather gnaw their own leg off than spend one more minute than necessary in the office. This seems the most obvious thing imaginable, but it amazes me how few companies do it.

And here's a thought: how much oxygen are you actually taking in? For a start, most people breathe very shallowly, using about the top third of their lungs. Lack of oxygen leads to them getting tired and emotional, which again contributes to the problem. Simply sitting quietly at one's desk and breathing deeply for a few minutes can have a remarkable effect on stress.

But let's put aside my feelings about the generic corporate culture for a moment and consider those more enlightened companies who feel that happy employees are more productive. Things can get interesting when a company switches its policy from battery farming to free-range. Trying to introduce a sunnier disposition to people trapped in a misery-sink can be something of an uphill battle, since employees may not trust the management and are still working in an environment that has stored their anger. This is why office refurbishment is a good way to start, but may not cure the problem entirely. Something obviously needs to be done to dispel the preceding atmosphere and give people a chance to face the new environment with a more open mind. Far Eastern companies have been doing this for years and have started to introduce the same approach here over the last twenty years or so. This has led to greater acceptance of such approaches as feng shui in corporate environments. The approach is effectively identical to that employed in the home, ensuring that positive energy can flow through the place harmoniously and can affect every member of staff. This has been shown to lead to a more comfortable and proactive business environment, as well as one that generates better results for the company and happier customers.

I am not a feng shui practitioner but I take a similar approach. I look at those areas where energy collects: break rooms, open-plan offices and suchlike, the places where people spend their time. Corridors are a means for getting from one place to another for energy as well as people and as long as they're kept clean and clear they shouldn't be a problem. Where I feel our approach has an advantage is that we're able to work effectively without being noticed. Normally, when we examine a corporate property, we are thought to be clients getting the tour because we're about to bring in a new account. It's also one of the reasons that the company has the name it does. Athanor Consulting could, in fact, do anything from IT to air conditioning – even someone who knows that Athanor is an old name for the alchemical furnace wouldn't necessarily connect that with the magical arts. Details like that help us to maintain discretion. Our approach is that nobody should know we've been there unless the client wants them to.

So we're looking at break rooms and offices – what are we looking for? The main thing we're doing is testing the atmosphere, working out where the negativity has settled and why.

Generally one doesn't see much in the way of aggressive phenomena because apathy and resentment are less likely to cause them than passionate anger. People rarely get passionate about office jobs, even when it comes to hating the boss, and passion is the kicker needed to make the really weird stuff happen. So what we normally find is the equivalent of stagnant pools, rather than raging fires. Once we know what the problems are, we address coping strategies: what is to be done to prevent reoccurrence of the same problems. We prefer to work with companies that are trying to change the pattern, although we are not unused to the idea of people who expect us to make their problems go away without doing anything about it themselves.

If we are working when the workplace is empty then we have a lot more space in which to work and can employ whichever techniques will get the job done most quickly. If the employees are still at work, then we tailor our methods to be as unobtrusive as possible. If required, we can operate in such a way as to be completely written off as a standard part of the workplace. Given the emphasis we place on discretion, it's hardly surprising that being effectively invisible is a popular choice.

The more obvious methods are the standard ones: they can involve incense, bells and all sorts of other aids to space clearing, but those tend to be done outside of office hours. When we come to operating 'under cover' the challenges begin. We employ energy filtering techniques based around breath work and meditation states that are designed to be quiet but effective. They just take a little more time. We're also able to use office conventions to our advantage: as long as you're dressed right it's amazing how far some people will go out of their way not to notice you, even if you're not wearing a pass, and the power of a clipboard to make one invisible is legendary.

Once we've neutralised the existing atmosphere, we recommend the company take steps to prevent it from building up again. Showing a more caring face is important: not just claiming that managers' doors are always open, but generating a more inclusive environment and giving employees a sense of their value to the company. Nobody likes to feel worthless and the tendency towards larger offices can easily give a sense that people are nothing more than tiny cogs in a big machine.

While I was revising this part of the manuscript before publication, someone suggested that people might find my own working environment to be of interest. My office at home in London (which is my main base of operations, separate from Athanor's office in Bristol) is small, untidy and contains several shelves of reference books (mainly on occult subjects – most of my books live elsewhere), a large amount of computer equipment, a sofa bed and a vast quantity of knick-knacks, mementoes and clutter. I know this bears little resemblance to my own recommendations, but the important thing to me in any work space is comfort and, even though my decorating tastes tend more towards the minimalist, it's an environment that I'm comfortable in. I know this makes me guilty of 'Do as I say, not as I do', but you'll notice a fair amount of that as we go through some of the cases that follow.

part two

WAR STORIES

chapter seven

SPOT CLEANING

Personal recommendations are always nice, even when they've come from a member of the team. This case came to us from Daniel, whose friend was having troubles and didn't know what to do about them. Fortunately, she mentioned them to him and he suggested giving us a call. This was one of Athanor's early cases, so an easy start was good for all of us, although it didn't give us any idea of what was going to follow as the years rolled by.

Daniel's been kind enough to explain the sight of us at work on a standard space-clearing, so that you can have an idea of how we work and how we deal with clients. Here is his account:

Daniel: I started the trouble on Christmas Day, 2000, really, because I began to wonder why it was that both the lamps in my friend Frances's office at home had failed in exactly the same way. She wanted me to change the bulb in one because she was sure it was going to fail soon and it was very difficult to get the bulbs out. The other lamp had broken too, because its fitting had failed. While we were working, two Zip disks failed and could not be recovered. I began putting two and two together. There had been no end of trouble with Fran's computer, the lights were failing and, above all, we both seemed to get very anxious in the room. I especially seemed to be getting very irritable but only when in that room.

I tried to assess the room and 'saw' a big patch of negative energy right by the desk. I thought I should clear the room out by ventilating it and fumigating it with incense, which I did. I moved the desk very gently, pushing it as slowly as I could. Things started to go very badly wrong. None of the equipment on the desk would work. I tried the fuse in the plug and changed it. This made no difference, although the original fuse had certainly blown. Still nothing worked. Frances insisted we try to plug it back in, using the original power point, but this made no difference either. All the power points appeared to be working perfectly.

I tried the fuse on the multi-plug and found that this had gone as well. I replaced it and this time we managed to get some power into the computer and it worked, as did the Internet connection. So far things were going well. I put a disk into the Zip drive and discovered that it wasn't working. Nothing happened. I checked the plug and put it into the power point directly. Still nothing happened. The fuse was dead. I replaced it and it immediately blew again. I replaced it a third time but still nothing happened. The whole thing was completely dead.

'Well, at least the computer is still working,' said Frances. Except that it wasn't. It had crashed and could not be restarted no matter what we did.

When I got home I felt awful. I rang Ian, although he was just heading for bed.

'I need your advice. I'll call you tomorrow night. If you're interested in a Christmas ghost story, I've got one for you,' I said.

'Oh, interesting,' he said. 'It's a deal.'

I went though an exercise for expelling negative energy and almost at once I started feeling a lot better. My calm returned and made me completely confident about things. The negative energy seemed to be affecting my mind rather than my body and I was surprised and shocked by the way it had been moving in Fran's room. The idea that it might be affected by gravity or behave like a fluid was extraordinary to me, but this was obviously what must have happened when I moved the desk in the office. It got stirred up, like muddy sediment at the bottom of a pool when you dabble your finger in the surface of the water. It would have got all over the room and caused the trouble. God knows how long the stuff had been there or how much damage it had already done. It did seem to be very difficult to shift.

The next day, I felt sick, had a splitting headache and felt depressed. I tried the technique for expelling negative energy again and, once more, immediately felt a lot better.

Ian rang me. He seemed so motivated towards getting the company moving and was even happy to use his magical talents for profit at last! I described the previous day's troubles to him.

'Have you come across anything like it before?' I asked.

'Oh yes, a couple of times, it sounds like it could be a curse. It's difficult to decide who it's directed against. It could be your friend or her dad, or you. I'll come down and have a look at it. I can trace the curse back and find out who laid it. I could come in and just blast it out of existence but that way you'd never know who it was who did it.'

We agreed a date the weekend after New Year. On Saturday, January 13, Ian Vincent and David Devereux came to London to help with the trouble in Frances's room. I met them at Piccadilly but Ian wanted to visit the British Museum first. The 'Dee Room' in the British Museum had been closed when he had been there before so he wanted to go back to see what they had relating to Dr John Dee. There were three small items, the wax disks he used to support his magic table and a small obsidian ball that had belonged to Horace Walpole (perhaps after it was Dee's). The obsidian mirror that Dee used as a scrying stone was not on display, which was a little disappointing. 'I've done a lot of work with that, remotely,' said Ian, 'and I wanted to see it in its context to "ground" it in reality.'

The two boys were dressed in 'team colours' – long black leather coats, and dark glasses. People around them certainly moved out of the way as they passed. I was wearing my long white overcoat, the same design as theirs, just cloth and white. I felt like the White Clown in the circus, the one who always stays apart from the action.

We got to Frances's house about a quarter past four and went upstairs to the guest room to have a talk over a cup of tea. Ian listened to Frances describing the history of the room, which used to be her father's study. He and David went in to have a look around. Ian then came back and told us that he felt it was not such a serious problem but there was a mass of negative energy in the room that had probably been there for a long time.

'It isn't directed at you or your dad,' said Ian. 'It may have come from one of the neighbouring houses, but some time ago. It's other people's toxic waste. Basically they've dumped it here and it's stayed here.'

He and David purified the room with sage and Ian probed with his pocket laser.

'It's something that isn't widely known in this business,' he said, 'but negative spirits hate coherent light.' He shone the laser at the mirror. 'Where does this mirror come from?'

'It was my grandmother's and I got it from my father,' Frances said.

'It's picked up some of the negative energy,' Ian said. 'You can see that the shadows are moving behind me even when I'm not moving, which is odd, and the laser is bouncing off in an unusual way.'

He finished the ceremony by casting a shield around the room to exclude the negative energy. 'It will just continue to spread out to the walls and push anything out with it.'

'Will I need to get it topped up later?' asked Frances.

'No, because it's rooted in the ground energy of the house so it's drawing its power source from the earth. There's no need to use your own energy because there's just so much of it free anyway.'

The room felt very different. When I came back in I realised that I had been accustomed to a slight drop in temperature on coming in which was now gone.

'Oh yes,' said Ian, 'temperature gradients are always a feature of this sort of thing.'

He was very pleased that it was not too serious, by his standards. 'On the "Richter Scale" this was a one point five,' he said. 'The one I did last week was about a four. I have handled a fifteen in the past, and don't forget the scale works on orders of magnitude!'

*

What's been described above is a textbook example of a space clearing. One isolates the cause, then deals with it as efficiently as possible. Not everything fights back, I'm happy to say, and most work in this area is accomplished quickly and easily with the right tools. The procedure is one that we use a lot, so I shall outline it here to save confusion when I refer to it later.

The primary methods we use for space clearing are smudge sticks, lasers, and breathing techniques. Smudge sticks are basically a specialised form of incense, invented by the native tribes of the south-western USA. Based on white sage, they can be obtained with a number of different ingredients, but, because we generally find the commercially available types don't quite match what we're looking for, we construct our own and take the opportunity to add a few refinements. Smoke is liberally distributed around the area to be cleared, sometimes with the aid of a fan, and the smoke helps to neutralise the energy in an area.

A laser can also be deployed during the process. These were observed by Ian a few years ago to be a useful tool for breaking up concentrated areas of energy, rendering them more susceptible to other techniques for dispersal. It can also be a useful technique for tackling such things as tulpas, since they have been observed to react badly to coherent light.

Breathing technique is described in chapter five but, to recap, the practitioner pulls in the negative energy with each intake of air and releases purified energy with the outward breath. How the removed energy is dealt with varies between practitioners.

Other, more aggressive, techniques for clearing a room involve deploying large amounts of energy in an intense, controlled burst to either drive out whatever may be present in an area or effectively incinerate it as though in a fireball. This is generally used to secure a working area quickly at the beginning of a job, to ensure a safe base from which to operate. These will be seen in action in chapter twelve.

If you're interested in John Dee, I've included a few notes on him and his work in the glossary.

chapter eight
MISFIRE

I was having a pint with a mate in a quiet little pub in suburban London. It's a thing that's all too rare in my life these days and thus it's a particular pleasure when I get to go with someone I've not seen for a while. He was just a regular mate, with no connection to the weirder side of my life, so it was a night of conversation, off-colour jokes and relaxed conviviality. I must admit I was a little surprised when he said he wanted my opinion on something work-related.

'I've got this friend...' he said.

This wasn't a surprise, since my friend is a popular sort of chap. But this friend of his had started acting out of character, and my friend was worried about him. So I asked what was happening and heard a tale of sleeplessness, strange dreams and a bizarre new obsession with always knowing what time it was. Now my first reaction was, understandably, to suggest he see a psychiatrist; it sounded to me like something had gone 'ping' in the guy's head and what he needed was a nice lie-down, a packet of happy pills and someone to talk to for a while. But no, said my friend. He knew that the chap in question had an interest in magic and the occult and had heard me talk about some of the risks involved with pursuing an interest in the subject, and thought that maybe something had gone wrong. I took some persuading but eventually caved in, making yet another mental note to try to stop my social life from getting involved with business. If he hadn't been so insistent, I would have turned him down flat and given him the office number, which, strictly speaking, is exactly what I should have done.

However, I had a call from my friend a couple of days later, saying he'd arranged to meet this guy for a drink and would I be able to join them? Since it meant free beer on his tab I agreed and wandered across to East London for a pint of the unusual.

I didn't like the guy the moment I set eyes on him. He was pale and had a drawn, sunken-eyed look about him that immediately made me think drugs. But I was there and I'd said I'd take a proper look, and I deserved at least a pint for hauling myself down to the pub at all. Not only that, my friend (we'll call him Andrew for the sake of convenience) had spotted me and was waving, so I was stuffed.

I grabbed a pint and went to join them at the table. Introductions were made, but without any mention of what I do. I'd insisted on that and was glad that Andrew was playing ball. We indulged in some idle chit-chat and I noticed that the unhealthy-looking guy, who I'll call Phil, was indeed looking at his watch uneasily every minute or so. I asked him what was up, but apparently nothing was so I let it go. Nearing the end of my pint, I claimed the need to visit the gents and stepped away from the table. This was a good excuse to get a look at Phil while he wasn't looking at me so, as I returned from the gents, I opened up and ran a scan on him from behind.

I can generally admit when I'm wrong and this was one of those times. While I'm not great at 'seeing auras' I could tell that this guy was seriously screwed up and if I hadn't been running with everything closed down to avoid attention I should have spotted it the moment I walked into the pub. He wasn't possessed or anything like that, but something had obviously happened to knock him pretty thoroughly sideways. Much to my annoyance, I resigned myself to the fact that it was something I could have a crack at dealing with and went about putting some kind of plan together.

When I got back to the table, I reached into my jacket for my wallet on the pretence that I was about to get a round in. As I pulled it out, I brought with it a copy of a popular magazine that deals with esoterica and strange occurrences that I'd picked up on the way there. This was Andrew's cue to play the introductory card:

'I didn't know you were into all that.'
'Yeah, well. I keep it pretty quiet.'
'Phil's into that, too. Aren't you, Phil?'

... And away we went. Andrew got more beers, saying he owed me a tenner anyway, while Phil and I started dancing around what we were interested in. I played it pretty low-key: an interest in Chaos Magic, that I'd tried a few sigils (*see* Glossary) and they'd gone OK. Nothing major and certainly no hints of what I did for a living. He admitted to an interest in Chaos as well, but he'd been working with more direct stuff to try and help his career in the City, which hadn't been going well. That was interesting, so I decided to play the interested newbie, work his ego a bit and get more out of him.

It worked like a charm, if you'll forgive the expression. One thing about magicians is that we tend to have pretty healthy egos. It's a tool we work with and self-confidence is essential if you're going to handle energy on any meaningful level. Once Phil thought he was the big man at the table, he was

The Zozo gun. This is a useful tool for focussing and concentrating a great deal of psychic energy into one short, sharp burst.

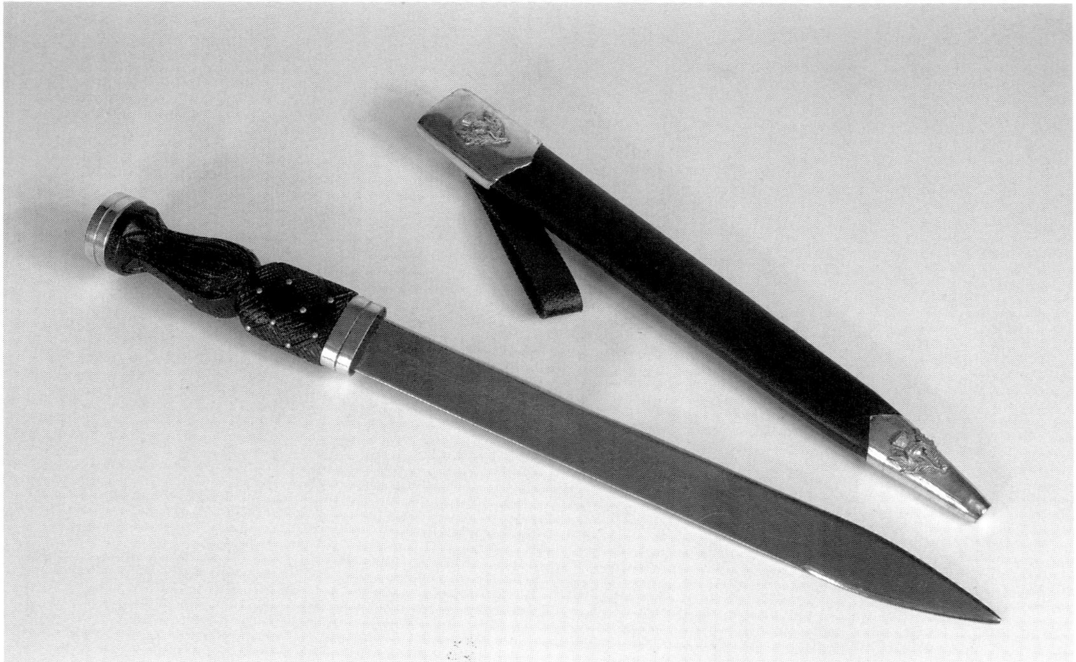

Originally bought to wear with a kilt, and rejected for that purpose since thistles are inappropriate for a Cornishman, this dirk now does duty as a ritual knife.

Smudge stick, with fan for aiding the distribution of smoke.

Every wizard has a staff, and this is mine. The stone that can be seen is believed to have originally been mounted on the pommel of an 18th Century Persian knife, and is usually covered by the brass cap.

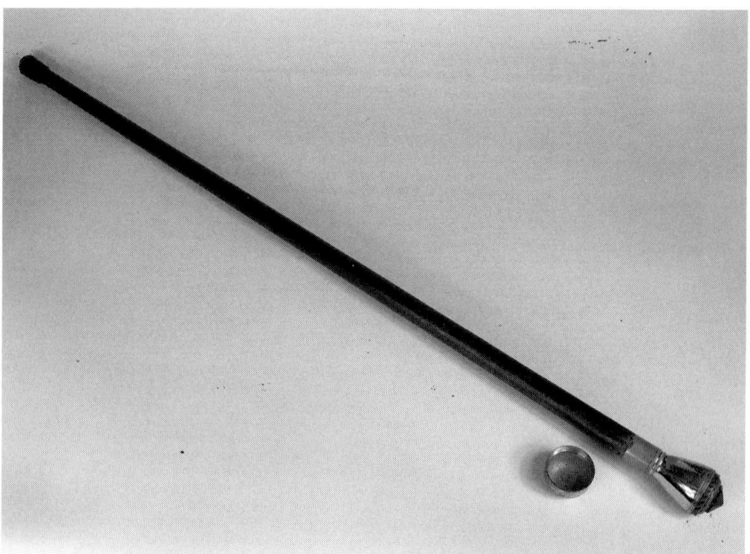

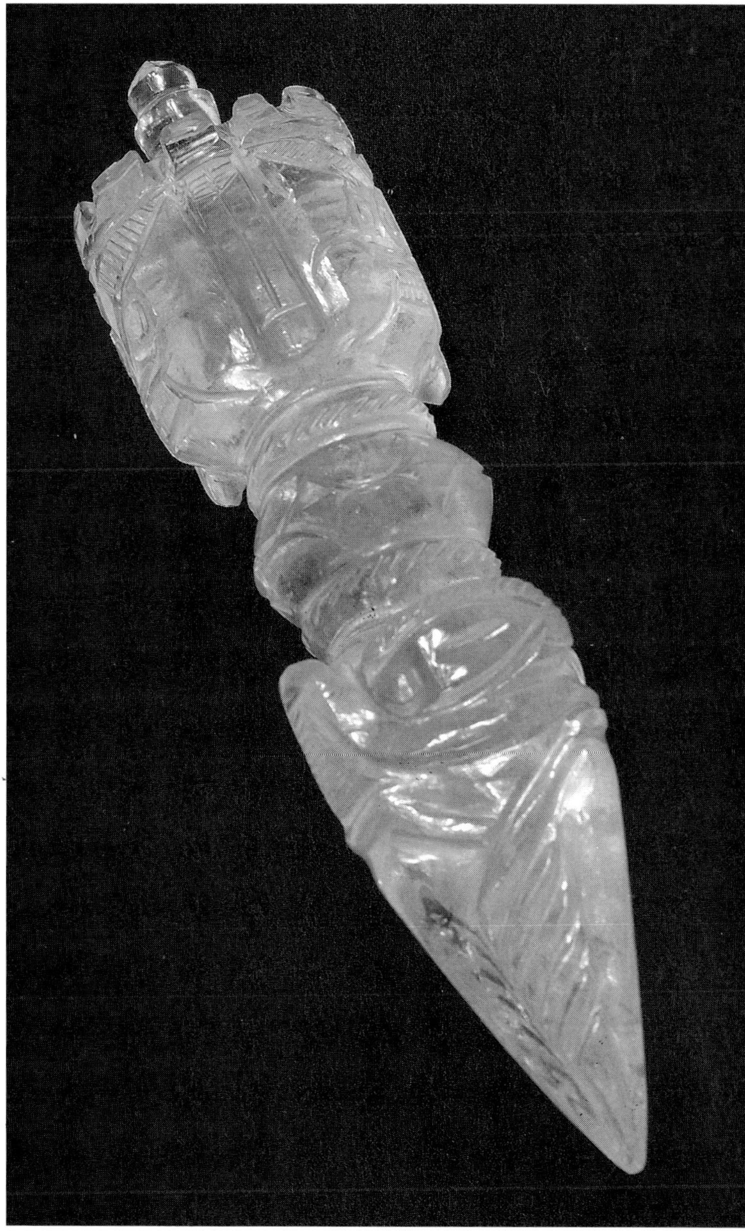

My phurba, a ritual knife used in Tibetan shamanism.
See the glossary for more information.

Left: The frontage of the Griffin Inn, Monmouth.

Below: The bar area of the Griffin.

Above: The 'Spider Mommy Cupboard' on the second floor of the Griffin Inn. The glass of water left to absorb any residual unpleasantness can be seen in the centre of the cupboard floor.

Below: Ian Vincent, founder of Athanor Consulting (left), with the author. (Photo: Kirsty Hall)

The Griffin Inn at Hallowe'en. The helmet / face shape that Tim refers to can be seen just to the left of the centre of the photograph, by shoulder of the woman wearing a black shirt. (Photo: Tim Gunter)

happy to wax a little more lyrical about his accomplishments. By the end of the evening he'd won me over a little, we were firm friends and had agreed to meet up for another drink.

The appointed day came around and I made my way back to the same pub – this time without Andrew. Phil seemed even edgier that before and certainly didn't look any healthier. We spent the evening discussing all sorts of the usual pub rubbish, as well as magic, and by the end I'd got him to invite me back to his place so he could lend me a book.

Phil actually seemed like a reasonably pleasant sort of bloke, even if he was a complete moron, and I didn't get any thrill out of suckering him in like this, but I was sure he wouldn't want to deal with me if he'd known from the start who I was.

So back we went to Phil's flat. It wasn't anything special, just another anonymous flat in an anonymous block, like so many all over London. I probably couldn't even find it again now if I went looking for it. But as I crossed the threshold I was hit by what's best described as a psychic wave that felt the way rotting meat smells. Something had gone seriously wrong here, and now I was in the mood to do something about it. The place was a mess – not that mess really means anything in and of itself – and not particularly well-lit or decorated. I could see a pile of washing-up by the kitchen sink that was in need of some serious attention and it was quite obvious from the general state of the place that Phil had been single for quite a time.

It was worse when we got into the living room. Judging from some of the kit on the shelves I surmised that this was where he'd been doing whatever it was that had started the trouble. There was a small collection of occult books, most of it pretty advanced stuff that could easily get an amateur into a lot of trouble, along with candles, a wand and chalice and a couple of ritual knives. Time to stop playing the idiot: I asked if he had an internet connection and pulled up the Athanor website for him to have a look at.

He hurled a tirade of abuse at me but I wasn't going to give him room to start trying to throw me out. I looked him straight in the eye and asked him exactly what the hell he'd been up to.

I think really he was glad of someone to tell, judging by the way that everything tumbled out once I'd knocked his righteous indignation off track. He had indeed been trying to help his career, but by cursing someone else who was in line for a promotion he wanted. He'd read a particularly nasty book (the availability of which is one of those down sides of the New Age revolution I mentioned earlier) and decided to try summoning one of the beasties listed therein. The trouble was that what he'd summoned was too big for him to handle and the whole thing had gone wrong, leaving him drained, plagued with dreams that made him afraid to sleep and convinced that he'd be dead in a few days. The way he was looking I could easily believe that last bit, if only because he was driving himself into the ground.

We had to fix this, and quickly. Casting an eye over his bookshelf, I noted that he had all the reference material I was likely to need and that there were candles aplenty. I quizzed him about what else he had in the house: incense, tools and so on. He had what I wanted, and a ton of other things, so I figured that I might as well get on with it.

I pulled a couple of books from the shelf, took the notebook from my pocket and started making notes. This was a one-shot job, but if I took the time to prepare the way I would normally then there might not have been enough time for things to settle themselves out afterwards. By the time I'd finished with the books, grabbed some printer paper and transferred what I needed onto it in nice big, easy-to-read letters, it must have been past two o'clock in the morning. Phil was in something of a state by this point, trying to work out a balance between being very pissed off with me, relieved that someone was helping and terrified by the idea of what I was about to do. While he might have been enough of a moron to mess with things he couldn't handle, he wasn't so stupid as not to recognise what I was setting up.

I had him help me set up the candles and prepare the incense and get the other trappings of a ritual together, then told him to get his ritual robes on. I don't bother with them and wouldn't have bothered with most of what we'd set up either, but Phil needed the dog and pony show to stabilise his head a bit and I can ham it up with the best of them when I need to.

With Phil dressed up, and my notes organised, I slipped my brain up a gear and started pulling energy together. My plan was only fairly dangerous as these things go, but I didn't want to risk dropping the ball when someone else's neck was on the line. Finally, I grabbed a nice big lump of obsidian from one of the shelves and stuck that into the smaller of the two areas we were about to work in. It was about three in the morning and I wanted it to be over and done by dawn.

I lit the candles and had Phil stand next to me, holding my notes up so I could see them. He'd been told not to move except as directed once I started and I was pretty sure I'd terrified him sufficiently to keep him in line. I was going Old School. Good old-fashioned, hardcore magic – straight out of Faust.

I started the opening part of the ritual and noticed from the corner of my eye that Phil's expression was getting less and less happy. I was bringing the circles online, setting up wards to make sure what we were summoning didn't have the chance to go anywhere. Once those were in place and looking good, I was ready to move into the next phase.

Summoning a demon, for that is what I was about to do, is by no means my idea of a fun way to spend an evening. Everything needs to be done properly and should generally be kept within the confines of one's system of choice. I'd set the room up with two circles: the larger one was my work area, and the smaller (where I'd left the obsidian) was where our guest would be arriving. Two circles are used to prevent the summoned creature from having a chance to get at you while you're working, since if it doesn't like what you have in mind it will more than likely try to stop you from doing it. Since I was about to pick an argument, I figured minimising its chances of doing anything to mess with my game was a pretty good idea.

So, with the candles lit, I chanted away, with Phil holding my notes up and making a pretty good go of not soiling himself with terror, and over in the other circle, the room got a little darker. We had established contact. I kept going with the ritual bits, giving the usual spiel about how powerful our invitee is, and how awesome and terrifying and generally amazing – your standard demonic PR, basically – and continuing to pull it through. After a few more minutes of this the air started to thicken and our demon, the one that Phil had previously messed up with, began to make his appearance. Short, squat, pale and ugly, with a nasty gleam in its eye, it was not that serious a demon as these things go but suitably malevolent for sending after people. At least it had turned up in a reasonable shape – two arms, two legs and only one head. It must have been feeling pretty good about showing up since the last time it was summoned here it had managed to have some fun with Phil.

I looked at the demon and the demon looked at me. Then

it looked at Phil, who was trying to work out if he was more afraid of the demon (which meant running away) or me (which meant not running anywhere near as far before I hit him), and finally back to me with a smile. It was expecting more of the same.

It was wrong.

(**Uncle Dave's Demonology Tip #1**: When addressing a demon, show some respect***. While you may be in charge of the situation, remember that the thing in front of you could be using your soul as a paperweight in two seconds flat should anything go wrong and you really don't want it to be upset. Do not, for example, behave as though you're guest starring in *The Sweeney*.)

I looked it up and down, then looked across to Phil, who had obviously decided that staying put was his best option (it was). I nodded towards the other circle and asked, 'Is that it?' Phil nodded.

'Really?' Another nod. 'You let *this* piece of shit get the better of you?'

This last comment didn't seem to be going down too well with our guest. I continued to ignore it.

'I should let it bloody well have you. This is embarrassing!' Over in the other circle, the demon was building up to something. I picked my moment, just before it was ready, and pointed straight at it. 'And as for you, you can bloody well sit still until I'm ready for you. You've caused me enough grief this evening as it is!'

Phil had gone white by now. He obviously wasn't familiar with the idea of browbeating things from elsewhere into submission and was expecting something to go horribly wrong at any second. As long as he stood still and stayed quiet, I couldn't have cared less. I must admit that I was a little bit angry at the mess he'd got himself into and, while the creature he'd tried to deal with wasn't exactly small fry, it wasn't really top drawer either. The best description I can give you would be a mid-level mob enforcer – no wimp, but hardly the Godfather. I figured it had had enough time to get slightly confused and rather annoyed by this point and was ready for the next stage. I rounded on it.

'Now then – you,' I said, lacing my voice with more than a touch of derision. 'What the fuck do you think you've been doing messing with my property?'

(**Uncle Dave's Demonology Tip #2**: Don't bother trying to bullshit a demon. They can generally see straight through you if they're thinking straight.)

It looked at me agog, as though it couldn't believe its ears. It answered in a snarl that echoed right through my head and would have cost thousands if you tried to get a synthesiser to reproduce it.

'Your property? This man is mine!'

'Bullshit.'

'What?' It had a look on its face that said it was having trouble getting its head round the situation. People as a rule don't summon demons to give them a bollocking and it really wasn't prepared for the way the situation was developing.

'This man is mine. Now either you fuck off and let it be, or I'm going to be even more pissed off than I already am.'

'It tried to bargain, it lost. It is mine now.'

'Really? I don't see your bloody mark on it.' I was getting into the swing of things by now, and the demon really hadn't got a clue how to deal with it. I decided to press my advantage. I looked at Phil, who now seemed to have decided that none of this was happening and had managed to relax a little. 'You. Whose are you? Your ass is mine, right?' He nodded. 'Did you give yourself to this lump of crap in the corner?' A shake of the head. 'Right. Glad that's sorted out then.'

'No. It is mine. It –'

'Shut up. It's mine. Now fuck off, will you, there's a good chap.'

'IT IS MINE!'

'No, it fucking well isn't! Are you as stupid as this is?' I indicated Phil with my head. 'Are you stupid enough to fight for it?'

'You are.'

'No, I'm pointing out your mistake. You've been pissing on my patch and I won't have that. Now either you can go back to whichever stygian depth you frequent when you're not trying to get one over on the amateurs, or you can stick around and get your ass kicked. Your choice, sunshine.'

It looked at me, obviously deciding on a course of action. Was it worth taking me on to keep a hold over Phil, or was it better to withdraw? Was I able to beat it in a straight fight as I'd suggested? Just how much of what I'd said was, in fact, rubbish? I stood my ground and let it look, since I really didn't have much of a choice in the matter. If I wanted out, I'd either have to break the circle and compromise the protections I'd carefully established or send the demon back and probably have to fight it down every step of the way. So I stood there, looking as pissed off as I sounded and giving every impression that I was ready, willing and able to crush it like an insect if it made me.

I have no idea how long this took. I'd taken my watch off before I started and couldn't see a clock from where I was. I was also a little concerned that if I'd started worrying about the time it might have taken that as a sign of weakness and we couldn't have that. My plan, such as it was, hinged on bullying the demon into submission rather than having to go toe-to-toe with it. I admit that it wasn't a very *good* plan, but there are times when all you can do is make a good guess and improvise from there on in. I was pretty sure that Phil wasn't exactly going to be my best friend even after I'd pulled him out of this. Some days you just do what you can and worry about the hoovering later.

After what seemed like an awfully long pause, the demon responded, 'No.'

'What?' My tone indicated that he might have just suggested dinner and a movie.

'It is mine and I shall have you as well.'

'Oh, bollocks. Are you sure about this?'

'Yes.' He was back on his own turf now, making a reasonable job of being menacing. 'You will be mine before I leave this place.'

I sighed. 'Wrong answer, dickhead. Now I've got to kick your arse.'

'You will not. You lie.' He'd obviously decided that I was trying to bullshit him with the easy attitude and the threats. Now I had to prove him wrong.

'Listen, sunshine. Let it go. Just piss off and everything'll be fine. Don't make me get nasty.'

But no, the demon wasn't having any of it. It was planning on going home with a twofer and no amount of threatening was going to persuade it otherwise. I was going to have to do this the hard way.

I turned to Phil, who was back to his terrified face, and selected a new page from the notes he was holding for me. He was holding his ground, though whether through confidence in my abilities or sheer terror was something he didn't look like he wanted to discuss at that particular moment. If

I'm going to be honest about it, I have to admit that I wasn't exactly feeling super-confident about this myself. I was stuck in a course of action I'd hoped to avoid, but whichever way it went I was 'Full speed ahead and damn the torpedoes', fired by the utter hatred of bullies I'd had since my childhood. Of course, it later occurred to me that in handling the job this way I was acting just like one.

'Last chance.' No response.

I started reading from the notes Phil was holding up for me, starting a ritual to bind the demon in place. Now the fight was on and I didn't want it running off to regroup. The air shimmered slightly around my target and it realised that it did indeed have something to worry about after all. It tried to withdraw, but I'd already got to the point where its access points had been closed and its only option was to fight. It was either going home with two souls, or not going home at all.

The room got colder suddenly and Phil let out a little whimper as the demon started to try a little magic of its own. I could feel the hairs standing up on the back of my neck and for a moment I had to watch my breathing to make sure I kept a level head. Deep, regular breaths are the secret of staying in charge. If you breathe faster, your heart rate goes up, if your heart rate goes up more adrenaline is produced, too much adrenaline makes you stop thinking straight. So deep level breaths and a calm voice, if only to keep myself believing that everything was fine and this was just another day at the office. I wasn't going anywhere I didn't want to go and wasn't doing anything I didn't want to do. Just a matter of keeping focused on the job at hand and not letting anything distract me.

Whatever the demon was trying obviously didn't work, because its confident smirk had been replaced by a vicious-looking glower. It snarled something incomprehensible (but quite probably unflattering) at me and then tried chanting something else. I wasn't planning on waiting to find out what that was, so I started the next phase of my plan. Turning another page, I started a chant of my own. I could see Phil starting to look a little dreamy-eyed, but since I'd started I had to keep going or it would blow the whole thing. I gave him a bit of a pat on the cheek, and that seemed to bring him back for the moment.

What I was doing was attempting to imprison the demon in the lump of obsidian. It's the same principle as trapping a genie in a bottle and makes them about as happy. Once the demon twigged what I was doing, it redoubled its efforts. Obviously deciding that Phil was the way to distract me, it seemed to be aiming to take him out of the picture. This was a good tactic, since if he fell across the border of the circle it would break a lot of the protections that I'd set up. Phil's eyes started to droop again and I pinched him hard enough to get a yelp. I'd hoped that he might realise what was happening, but he was either so far gone or sufficiently stupid to seem really annoyed at what I'd done. I could see he was about to say something, but I managed to silence him with a frown as I got to the end of the passage. The obsidian had been set up to receive the demon. Now all I had to do was get the bastard in there.

As with so many things in magic, this was much easier said than done. The demon, now fully aware of what I was doing, looked as though it was marshalling itself for one last big push, to break my hold and provide a means of escape even if it meant losing its hold on Phil. This was now effectively a game of survival for the demon, since it knew I wasn't likely to let it out any time soon.

As I took a breath ready to begin, Phil fainted. Just like that, his eyes slammed shut and he dropped like a sack of potatoes. I caught him as he dropped and just about managed to arrange for him to land (somewhat folded up) inside the circle. I should have expected something like that, but we didn't have a lot of space to work with and I'd actually expected the demon to back down rather than risk slugging it out with me.

(**Uncle Dave's Most Important Demonology Tip**: Make sure you can back up your threats.)

I grabbed my notes from underneath Phil's ribcage and went for it. Unfamiliar phrases in Enochian (*see* Glossary) flowed far better than they usually do and I threw every ounce of energy I could spare into stuffing this demon into the piece of rock that was just inside its circle. Realising now that it was beaten, its aggressive attitude switched to pleading, begging for mercy, for release. It was promising to go and never come back, to release Phil, to give me anything I wanted – power, money, women, whatever I could think of. It would be my servant, it would do anything, if I just let it go.

It wasn't going anywhere but into that lump of obsidian. I knew very well that I wouldn't be able to trust it, that it would do everything it could to twist my wishes in such a way as to make me miserable, or worse.

As I neared the end, I could see what looked like the top of the rock opening up much wider than it had any right to if physical laws were involved, and a huge dark space inside it, seeming to swirl like a whirlpool. The demon seemed to be feeling some kind of pull from it, as it changed position as though trying to brace against a wind. Then there was a moment where the demon seemed to stretch like modelling clay in the direction of the stone, the half closest to the rock stretching towards it as the half facing away stayed perfectly formed. Less than a second later, the demon was gone and the rock looked perfectly normal again. There was a roaring in my ears and I realised I was panting as though I'd just run a hundred-metre sprint. My heart was beating like a hammer in my chest and I was drenched in sweat. But nothing was in the room with me except Phil, curled up at my feet.

Carefully, I opened my senses out to check for anything in the room. All I got was the lump of obsidian, now obviously holding the demon, radiating in a very unpleasant manner indeed.

I'd managed to pull it off. I'd won.

Gingerly, I closed down the circles I'd been using and made sure there wasn't any mess left behind. Then I picked up the lump of obsidian, wrapped it in my handkerchief and put it in my pocket. Finally I found the kitchen, made a cup of tea and helped myself to a large glass of cheap vodka to steady myself a bit.

I woke Phil up with a glass of water and informed him that I'd be sleeping on the floor. He was going to let me have the piece of obsidian, too, and if I heard even the merest whisper on the grapevine that he was trying to do anything like that again I was going to kick his arse to Moscow and back. He was out of the black magic business and he'd do well to avoid being anywhere near me for some length of time. Then I sent him to bed, waited for the snoring to start and lay down on the sofa. I was asleep in seconds.

I woke up somewhere around lunchtime, to discover that Phil was still snoring in the bedroom. I let myself out into an overcast world and went in search of a greasy spoon: I needed breakfast.

*

I think in this case that it's important that I say something about the way I dealt with what was going on. My plan was both dangerous and stupid and could have gone wrong at several points along the line. In fact, of the all the dangerous, dumb-ass things I've done in my life, this was probably the dumbest. Most magicians, especially ones with experience of working in this field, will tell you not to try anything like this and so would I. I'd certainly be inclined to consider an awful lot of alternatives before I tried it again.

I've said it before and I'll say it again: research and backup are your friends. Working as a lone wolf is a great way to get your head handed to you on a plate. I'd really rather not think about what might have happened if it had gone wrong.

chapter nine

RIGHTING RITES

A lot of our clients find us via the internet and this one was no exception. An urban professional, she'd done everything she could to find an explanation for what was happening in her flat, but without success. In desperation, she remembered an article she'd read in a magazine about someone who deals with this sort of thing and went to her favourite web search engine. Having considered the options, she came to us.

A single professional in her early thirties, the client lived in a flat in a fairly pleasant suburb of London. Since moving in about eighteen months previously she had experienced strange dreams, out-of-character mood swings and occasionally noticed movements out of the corner of her eye. She was becoming tired and her work was starting to suffer as a result. Since her job involved other people's money she was naturally concerned about her responsibility to her clients and colleagues as well as her own position and she felt that, if something wasn't done to resolve the situation soon, then things would start to go downhill very quickly.

Further questioning revealed little to give us any clues. Her building dated from the late nineteenth century, and had been flats for an unspecified amount of time. We couldn't find any history for the building beyond what the client knew about the previous owners, a young couple who'd needed a bigger place to start a family. The client had had no previous interest in, or contact with, the paranormal or occult and would normally have laughed at the suggestion that it was a possible cause of her problems. She was even honest enough to say that she felt foolish coming to us at all and that she hoped we'd say her problem had another cause entirely.

I met Ian at Paddington and we had our standard pre-job meeting in a café near the station, running through the information we had and our opinions and impressions of what we'd been told. It sounded like an interesting case, nothing too unusual from our perspective, but the client's natural scepticism worked in our favour as she'd already eliminated most of the more prosaic causes we'd normally consider. The plumbing had been checked, the central heating serviced and the flat redecorated all within the preceding twelve months, which was after she'd started noticing that things were wrong.

With food in our bellies and our work heads on, we made our way to the flat. First impressions of the building didn't reveal much of interest. Although we were able to spot which floor she lived on there didn't seem much to see from the outside. So we walked up to the main entrance and rang the bell. We were buzzed in and took the stairs rather than the lift, just in case. It wouldn't have done to get caught in the lift, although we hadn't been told of any reason to worry about that.

When the client let us in we got down to business pretty quickly. There wasn't much to add to the questionnaire, she'd made a point of telling us everything she could remember and had even gone so far as to email us with one extra detail when it had come to her. So, it was time to look over the flat and see what was what.

We had been sitting in the front room, comfortably-sized and decorated in a relaxed fashion with lots of books on the end wall. Directly across the corridor lay the kitchen and turning right, away from the front door, took us down to the bathroom and two bedrooms – the smaller of which was obviously used as a home office.

Our point of interest was definitely the bedroom. Conservatively furnished and extremely tidy, it was noticeably cooler than the rest of the house. Since the heating had been recently serviced and the room was double-glazed, the client was at something of a loss to explain this when we remarked on it but, given the feel of the room, it wasn't a surprise to us. While there had been a background of something in the front room, it was much stronger here and this was obviously the centre of the activity. When we asked, the client mentioned that she'd tried sleeping in the other bedroom with fewer bad dreams as a result, but not enough to make it worth moving things around. Also, she needed to concentrate in her office and was afraid that she wouldn't work as well if she had to work in what was now her bedroom.

The way the energy was flowing in the bedroom seemed weird – a mixture of latent negativity with a distinct edge of something. It was just a matter of putting my finger on it. I conferred with Ian; he was getting the same feeling, but he recognised it. Someone had been messing around with Tantra (*see* Glossary) and not very well. Whatever they'd been doing had sparked off on something already there and gone wrong and they hadn't done anything to clear up the mess. So now it was just a matter of separating the energies out and dealing with them individually.

The first part of that was going to be Ian's job. He's our resident expert on Tantra, so my part would be to watch his back and feed him extra energy if he needed it. He slipped off his shoes and sat cross-legged on the bed, settling into a comfortable position for the meditation to come. He started to breathe.

Watching Ian breathe is an experience. He's a big lad, but the sheer amount of air he can move when he gets going is a sight to behold. The client was certainly impressed and as he started to work I could feel the atmosphere charging and starting to change under his direction. It took him a while, but he was able to bring the energy level down and wrap it up to the point where I could get a better idea of what else was going on. With Ian's part done, I spotted it right away – death, and not a happy one.

We broke for coffee and explained to the client what we'd done so far and what was going to happen next. She listened to us with an expression that told us she wouldn't have believed a word of it if she weren't already seeing results.

Then it was my turn to work. I went back into the bedroom and started pacing, getting a feel for what was happening there and, just as importantly, what had started it. Not a natural death, certainly. Just a matter of feeling it, getting an idea of the flavour. Just relax and let it come. There was an edge of despair, a sadness that had lost its way. No anger, no hate – no directed hate, anyway. Suicide.

There was no sense of the person still being here, so it was just a matter of dealing with the emotions released in death. Not too complicated, then, although it would probably leave me miserable for the rest of the week.

I looked at my options. I could either release it, convert it, or lock it away in an object for later release somewhere safer. Given that the client had really suffered enough, I decided to go for option three. I checked my briefcase for something suitable and came up with one of the miniature bottles of rum

I tend to carry in my kit for moments when I need an emergency libation. That would do nicely. I poured half of into my coffee cup for afterwards and went back to work.

I placed the open bottle on the dressing table, with the cap beside it as Ian took up position in the doorway to keep an eye on me, while I sat down on the bed. It was simply a matter of getting an idea of the shape of the thing, then concentrating it down and remoulding it to fit in the bottle, where the rum would hold it in suspension. All I had to do was relax…

This is bloody hard to do when your heart rate's up and you've got a shedload of Italy's finest dark roast rolling round your system. It's an art. Just a matter of stepping away from your adrenal glands for a moment and letting the body do its thing while you get on with the job in hand. Breathing, focus and an awful lot of practice. I let my mind drift for a moment, feeling the room around me and the energy as it moved around the room. Then, once I'd got the hang of it, I started to push. Gently at first, moving the current so it slipped closer to the bottle with each cycle. Interrupting the flow just past it so that a little slipped inside. It was easier for me this way, making gradual changes rather than just trying to stuff it all in at once. With a bigger bottle I could have got away with less finesse, but that was what I had to work with, so that's what I did.

Once I'd got it rolling, things went fairly smoothly. I could see the rum starting to darken a little and another gentle push sent a larger amount of the energy into the bottle with each tap. It took about half an hour, but eventually the room was clear and the bottle looked considerably less appetising than it had before. I stood up, walked over to the dressing table and screwed the cap onto the bottle. Ian stepped into the room and checked to see how I was, then opened up to sense the room to see how I'd done. I knew before he told me that I hadn't got all of it and that I'd have to deal with the rest another way, but I already had a plan for that.

Ian went back to his position while I prepared myself for the next phase. I still didn't want any release going on for the sake of the client, so I was going to trap it another way temporarily and release it off the premises. I centred myself again and reached out to feel the energy still flowing through the room. There was barely a tenth of what had been before, which I knew was well within my ability to handle – especially for the short period of time I had in mind. Again I started pushing the current, shaping its pattern to take it where I wanted it to go. A shiver ran through my body as it hit me and with each inward breath I took a little inside me. I couldn't tell you how many breaths it needed, or how long, but eventually I was filled with despair, tired of life and wanted nothing more than for it all to end. I looked over to Ian, who nodded to confirm that I had it all. Then he stepped aside as I came out of the bedroom, went into the bathroom, lifted the toilet seat and puked my guts out. With each heave I pushed out as much of the despair as I could and by the time I was down to stomach acid the feeling had left me. I flushed and asked Ian to check the room and clear up any of the energy that might have escaped my purging. While he did that I washed my mouth out with rum. It might not have been minty fresh, but it got most of the vomit flavour out.

This had left the client somewhat bemused. I'm not sure what she'd been expecting, but I'm willing to bet it wasn't heavy breathing and vomit. Still, we'd certainly had an effect on the room and it was warming up already to match the rest of the flat. We decided to give the rest of the place a going over, just to stabilise things across the board and make sure we left things in as good a shape as possible. Standard space-clearing techniques with a smudge stick from Ian's kit bag yielded good results, and we left a very happy client in our wake, promising to recommend us to her friends.

chapter ten

FIRE AND WATER

There were four residents in the house: the client, her husband, their son and his girlfriend, who was treated as another member of the family and enjoyed an excellent relationship with her beau's parents. They'd lived in the house for fifteen months at the point where they contacted us and were obviously distressed by the pattern of misfortune. This was the last attempt they were going to make to render the house habitable before reluctantly having to consider selling the place and moving somewhere less troublesome.

The trouble had started on the day they moved in with a flood in one of the house's outbuildings. This was serious in itself, but made much more so by the large amount of wiring that ran through that particular building and had been immersed in the flood. A plumber was called to pump it out, but the water was back within a couple of hours. One of their dogs was also very ill that evening, vomiting all over the client's husband at one point.

They also noticed that the ceramic tiles in the main entrance hall had been polished in such a way as to make them exceptionally slippery, which had hampered the moving in somewhat and had to be rectified by a professional cleaning company as it was impossible to remove the polish by normal domestic means. This wasn't a supernatural event, but didn't exactly make them feel welcome.

Purchasing the property at all had been extremely difficult and had required extensive professional assistance. The previous owner, a German gentleman, had been forced by circumstances to sell and had done everything possible to prevent, or at least delay, the sale. It also appeared that he had not enjoyed good relations with his neighbours. There had been a long-running boundary dispute (for which he seems to have billed his neighbour at one point) and those acquainted with him had nothing good to say about him when they spoke to the new occupants of the house. It was also our client's understanding that the house had been rented out for a goodly proportion of its time in his ownership.

The gentleman's wife had also told them things that turned out to be untrue. Most notably, they had been assured that the swimming pool was in full working order and that ventilation was adequate to prevent any difficulties with condensation. Sadly, this had not been the case, and required a great deal of trouble, and money, to rectify.

Almost as soon as the work was complete, there was a fire. Fortunately, no one was hurt and everything was insured, but there was a fair amount of damage to put right – again. The forensic investigation found the cause to be a piece of plastic ball hidden under the sauna, next to the swimming pool. Work to repair the damage was supposed to take three months, but a succession of difficulties meant that work was still continuing when they contacted us eight months after it had begun (and was in fact still underway when we visited), with at least another month to go. This was despite having taken the trouble to employ a reputable firm of builders and a surveyor to manage the work. No matter what they tried, things were constantly happening to set them back, even to the point of a delivery lorry crashing into their house's front gates.

Shortly after the fire had happened, they employed the services of a Feng Shui consultant from a reputable London firm. Having spent some time examining the premises, she advised selling the house and moving, as corrective action would be extremely expensive. Nonetheless, the clients decided to try the improvements that were recommended. This work was still ongoing when the client contacted us, delayed again by a multiplicity of problems.

The problems weren't just structural, either. A griddle in the kitchen seemed to turn itself on twice, filling the kitchen with smoke. The oven stopped working on Christmas Eve, causing any amount of trouble, and yet was perfectly functional when an engineer came to repair it. Fuses on household appliances were blowing with a disturbing frequency, almost causing another fire on one occasion, and other equipment was refusing to work at random intervals.

The client, having catalogued their misfortunes, ended her email with the wonderfully phlegmatic 'I think you will agree that there are too many things going wrong for it to be normal'. Oddly enough, we did. And along we went.

It was a nice house, built in the 1960s and mostly on one level, sitting in front of a gravel drive with a garage to the left. A smallish pile of building refuse sat opposite the house on the other side of the drive. To our right was a lawn, with trees beyond it, and in front was the client, coming out to meet us as we unloaded our gear from the car.

She led us into the house, past signs of the continuing building work and sections that were masked off with plastic sheeting, and then into a fantastic living room that was large, light and airy with French windows running the length of it on the garden side. A spiral staircase led up to a balcony on the upper floor and a wide opening led into the kitchen. The furniture was tasteful and the TV and audio equipment was first class. We sat in the kitchen for coffee and chatted for a while with the client, her son and his girlfriend, getting more information about the previous owner and what had happened since they'd moved in.

We were disappointed that the Feng Shui consultant they'd used hadn't left them a written report, which I would have expected. It wasn't too important for us – no background data meant no clues of what to look for but at least it would be a clean scan. My main disappointment was more for the client: she'd spent a fair amount of money getting a reputable professional in and been rewarded with nothing more than the suggestion that they move. This also struck me as irresponsible, pushing the problem onto someone who wouldn't know the history of the place rather than doing something about it.

While I have a certain amount of respect for Feng Shui, in that I agree with the concept of energy flow through a house, I'm not as convinced as some others as to its general efficacy. Some of the concepts simply don't translate. For example, south is considered an important direction because the Emperor used to live in the north and thus his gaze would be facing south as he watched over China. This doesn't seem quite so relevant in Chipping Sodbury, or in Reykjavik.

We scanned the family as we talked, finding nothing more than stress and low-level exhaustion, which was a good start. I stepped outside for a cigarette and got a feel of the garden. It felt like good ground: this wasn't a problem with the area, or anything outside the house. The family were good people, too. There was a real bond between them, which was nice. I mentioned the feel of the garden to Ian and Jane when I got back inside and my feeling that whatever we were hunting was going to be inside the house.

Ian had unpacked the video camera by this point, so we guessed that the best thing we could do was start the walk-through. Senses open, starting to get a feel for the place, we walked slowly around the ground floor, past rooms where builders were still at work. There was what looked as though it would make a fine drawing room complete with fireplace (and workmen fixing it up), plus an office, an exercise room and several rooms that were obviously still being renovated after the fire. Once all this work was finished, it was going to be a really nice place to live, as long as we took care of whatever was causing the trouble. Up to the first floor, where the sleeping quarters faced each other across the balcony. A left turn first, through a room being used to store things during the building work and then into the client's bedroom. Out of there, across the balcony and into the son's area. A workroom to the right, with music gear, and bedroom ahead. Finally, out of there and back to the kitchen, then to the pool.

The pool was empty and obviously still being repaired. We took a look at the sauna and the storage area, nodding to the workmen as we passed. Another advantage of wearing suits when attending clients is that builders just think you're a surveyor or something.

The sauna had a distinctly unpleasant feeling, like a bad smell hanging around, and was colder than its surroundings. The pool was equally nasty. It had been drained and both Ian and I felt a pull towards it, as though it wanted us to think it was full of water and that we really wanted to dive in and have a nice swim. We both managed to shrug it off, but we were surprised somebody hadn't already decided to try diving in and landed head-first on the tiles eight feet below.

What was interesting was that the whole house had the same kind of nasty background read. While the pool was unpleasant, it didn't stand out sufficiently for us to point to it as a source of the trouble and nor did anywhere else. Odd. We turned to Jane, who is by far the best of us when it comes to communication and has an excellent knack for seeing through to the root causes of things, to see if she could put her finger on what was happening.

Jane's thought on the matter took us back to the gentleman who'd owned the place previously. Was it worth looking at his resentment at having to sell the place as a cause? It would certainly provide a model for the family being sabotaged at every step and made to feel uneasy and unwelcome in their own home.

But that needed confirmation, which meant we had to check outside. The son, who was quite interested in how we worked, accompanied Ian and myself as we took a walk around the perimeter of the property, around the garden, over the rockery at the back of the pond and into the woods. Once we'd lost sight of the house, we came upon a scene that unsettled me for a second. It was a largish clearing, about twenty feet across, with a single chair standing upright in the middle, which the son told us was left over from the fire and had no reason to be there at all. Something about it just struck me as *wrong*, like a scene from a Japanese horror film. However, just as all that glitters ain't gold, not everything that looks spooky actually is. While it was a momentarily freaky thing to see, there was no atmosphere to back it up. We found a second, smaller clearing a little further on and I made a note of this, as it struck me that the second clearing might come in useful later on.

Jane's comment on the grounds was simple: 'The place *wants* this sorted'. Ian and I agreed, since we'd both got a similar feeling but with nowhere near the intensity Jane had. This confirmed our initial thoughts from the house itself. If the old man's anger had permeated the place so much as to affect the new owners, then it was a problem that we knew the solution to. We were going to shake it loose.

Normally, we'd be able to do that fairly simply, but in this case the old man had so thoroughly poisoned the place that we were going to have to use some fairly extreme measures. We also wanted to be sure that we got it in one hit, in case it was going to try making a fight of it. Since 'heavy weapons' tend to be my field, I gave it some thought over another cigarette.

I decided that the best way to do this was with a shock wave or two. I'd start by shaking the house's psychic field from the inside, using the same remote techniques one would use for delivering a psychic attack, only with the type of energy burst used for clearing a space quickly. As soon as that had happened, I'd do the same thing from the outside by hitting it simultaneously from all directions. A carefully constructed network of shield walls would bounce everything we set loose straight to a mirror in the exercise room, where Ian would be waiting to catch it with another shield construct. I'd then come back in and take the final shot to terminate it.

While Jane stayed with the family, Ian and I decided on the pattern of charges. Essentially, these are packets of psychic energy that sit quietly until triggered, then burst like an explosive. It took a while for us to work out the right pattern of charges and shields to get the effect we were looking for. We paid particular attention to the pool area because of its history, but by the time we were done we were as sure as we could be that whatever was causing the trouble only had one place to go – straight into Ian's waiting arms.

Next came the preparation outside. Remembering that second clearing, I decided that that would make a perfect work area for me. Since I wanted to be outside the blast area when it went off, that meant working round the border between the garden and the woods and then following an orbit around the house at roughly the same distance. The route got a little bumpy at times, taking me over the rockery again and through some of the areas that the builders had been using to dump waste material, but my usual policy of wearing solid boots to work rather than formal shoes has stood me in good stead before and did here again. I used a slightly different technique here on the outside, planting charges that would absorb local energy and use that for the burst rather than any more than a token amount of energy from my own reserves. It doesn't take any physical props to do this, just a couple of seconds' concentration and a quick visualisation. I was doing it this way because I was using an awfully large number of charges (one every couple of metres over quite an extensive perimeter) and working on the theory that if the land that the house was sitting on wanted it sorted that badly then it could bloody well help out!

Jane reported a marvellous interlude from the kitchen while I was outside:

Client: 'He looks serious.'
Son: 'He is.'

I came back in and explained to Ian and Jane what I'd done, then Jane translated what I'd said for the clients. I confess that sometimes when I'm focused on a job I forget that not everyone speaks Devereux, so Jane fills a wonderful role of converting my short, slang-filled utterances into English. We think it's much better to explain each stage of what we're doing to the client, rather than just talking among ourselves. Considering that they're our reason for being there and our first point of information, it makes good sense to make them feel included in the process.

We discussed what everyone was going to do, then took up positions. Jane sat with the family, shielding the group, and I accompanied Ian as he went to the exercise room, ready to catch what we shook loose. It was time to start the countdown: five minutes.

I checked with Jane as I passed, warning her that she was close to the pool, where rather a lot of activity was about to happen, and to shield particularly well in that direction. Four minutes.

I walked out of the house and into the garden. I was working myself up, getting my focus organised and preparing for what was to come. Across the lawn to the edge of the woods, and three minutes to go.

Into the woods, keeping an eye on the countdown and trying not to fall over the bracken underfoot, which would have possibly screwed up the timing and made me look like an idiot. Two minutes.

I got to the clearing and found a comfortable place to stand. There was still a minute to go, so I ran through a breathing exercise and focused. Next, I reached out to feel the charges that were placed inside the house, checking that they were good to go. Then I checked the outside charges, which were equally ready. With fifteen seconds to go, I threw up the heaviest shield I could. I wasn't expecting to catch any backwash, but I didn't want to be thrown off in the next phase of the job. Then I started the countdown out loud from ten. At five, I closed my eyes, ready to kick things off. Three, two, one… I took a breath, smiled, and said what felt right at the time.

'Fire in the hole.'

I could almost hear the bang as the charges in the house went off and the birds stopped singing. As the blast wave started to expand, I hit the second set of charges and the ring around the house blasted straight back inwards. Everything was going as planned.

Stepping out of the clearing, I could hear the birds starting to sing again as I walked back across the lawn and back into the house. I walked straight past Jane and the family, who looked a touch shell-shocked, and on to the exercise room. My phurba (*see* Glossary) was already in my hand and I was buzzing with energy, ready for whatever Ian had managed to catch. As I walked around the corner, I could see he had something but didn't even bother to look at what it was: if it was friendly, he wouldn't be holding it like that. I raised my arm, took aim and let loose with a blast of energy.

I looked again and it was gone. Ian was looking at me as if I'd just used a hand grenade on a butterfly and I checked to make sure he was OK. Obviously I'd been a bit more stoked than I thought. We went back to the kitchen where Jane was sitting with the family to make sure that everyone was OK. I didn't doubt Jane's ability to shield everyone, I just wanted to see how things were.

Things were, of course, fine. The atmosphere was a lot clearer, too, clear enough for Jane to point out that the kitchen was an extension and that she was sitting a couple of feet from what used to be the back door of the house. The client confirmed this with a look of surprise. Jane went on to voice her opinion that some enormous argument had taken place on the spot, possibly between the old man and a neighbour, leading to a serious enmity. Bearing the border dispute in mind, that didn't surprise any of us particularly, but it was a nice indicator that we'd shifted the crud that was previously making things unpleasant. We decided to do a full space-clearing of the house, just to be sure that nothing came back.

Ian and I took half the house each and set forth with

smudge sticks to give a little extra edge in case it was needed. It was a fairly simple walk-through for me, and I wasn't picking anything up at all as I cleared my part of the house and collapsed the shields that we'd set up as buffers. This was enough to finally put a smile on my face after my earlier exertions, which had left me with a pretty grim aspect. I was glad to get that grim mood over and done with because, while it's necessary sometimes for me to let my ruthless streak loose, it does tend to unnerve clients. In fact, I tend to have a pair of sunglasses handy for times like this and for scanning people, since I've had one too many comments about freaking people out. If they can't see my eyes, apparently it's a lot easier to deal with.

Next, we decided to check the outside buildings. The builders had left at some point while I hadn't been paying attention, so we were able to wander freely and check for anything we didn't like the look of. The only area that seemed to need attention was the pile of debris on the other side of the house from the driveway, which turned out to have been cleared from the fire. This felt more like residual than active unpleasantness, but we treated it carefully and made sure we removed it thoroughly.

We sat and had a coffee with the family, chatting about normal things now that we'd finished the job. It's a good way to help people deal with what's happened. Having us round for an afternoon is not the sort of experience most people consider an everyday thing and this is a good way to remind them that we're still ordinary people even if what we do is quite unusual. Of course, we were still monitoring the situation, and the family, to make sure that everything was OK and they remained as happy as they seemed. The house certainly felt better and they were looking as though a weight had lifted from their shoulders. When that had continued for another half hour we decided it was time to pack up the kit and make our way home, me back to London, and the rest to Bristol.

I got a phone call from Ian a couple of days later. He'd had an email from the client to say that things were starting to feel a little weird again and would I mind taking a look? The son's girlfriend had also become suddenly unwell, primarily with acute asthma, so Ian was going to see what he could do for her while I checked the building.

I retired to my work room, relaxed, and focused on my destination. It was pretty easy to get a lock on the house, given that I'd been there so recently and there were still slight traces of our work there, so in what seemed like only a few seconds I was standing on the balcony overlooking the living room. I had a sense of something behind me, in the son's quarters that he shared with his girlfriend, directly over the kitchen. Turning, walking down the corridor I'd been in only a couple of days before, I could see the problem in the far corner of the room, sitting like a dark mist. A small amount of negative energy, that was probably going to do its best to grow back and cause more mayhem. It was a fairly simple procedure to crack out the virtual flamethrower and incinerate the lot.

I decided to do a quick check over the rest of the house since I was there and found nothing else to worry me, so I pulled back out and called Ian to compare notes. I told him what I'd found and how I'd dealt with it and he sent an email back to the client letting her know that we'd dealt with what had been worrying her.

There were the usual follow-ups made and the family reported that all was well. To my knowledge they're still living there and everything continues to be in good order.

chapter eleven

UNWELCOME PASSENGERS

Not all cases go as planned. Sometimes we do all we can for somebody, but their lack of cooperation gets in the way of the process. When we accept a case, it is made very clear that the client will need to do their part to help us get the job done. It's not like calling in a washing machine repair man, then sitting back and letting them take care of it. We need to know stuff, we need to get a look around the areas not affected by the problem as well as the ones that are and we need to get as much information as we can. That generally means that we'll want to talk to everyone involved. We don't think it's that much to ask, but we can work around it as long as we are told everything there is to know about a situation. A lack of data means a loss of efficiency. We don't deny it; in fact we stress it to our clients during the research phase as often as we can.

This case begins in a rural location. A farmer contacted us asking for help. His house had been built five years before on the site of a 1901 house that was in turn built on an even earlier foundation. All remains from the previous buildings had been removed during the construction and were now elsewhere on the property. The farmer and his family had lived on the site for over fifteen years. He described their fortunes as 'mixed' since moving there and his wife had decided to visit a clairvoyant some time previous to the new house being built. The clairvoyant had told them that there was a presence in the house that held some kind of grudge against them.

When the new house was being constructed, access was discovered to a cellar of which the client had no previous knowledge and that was not shown in any previous surveys of the property. The clairvoyant visited again and gave her opinion that the malign presence was in the cellar and indeed experienced some difficulty in leaving the area after examining it. The lock on the cellar door jammed so securely that it needed to be disassembled and she reported the feeling of someone trying to push her back down the stairs.

The client's wife also reported the feeling of being surrounded by a cold, dark cloud while in the basement one evening and of hearing footsteps above on more than one occasion when, on investigation, she proved to be the only person in the house.

There was also a report from the client's eldest son, who was in his mid-thirties. He was unable to go into the cellar at all, experiencing breathing difficulties whenever he tried. The client himself said that he could feel something, but it did not seem to affect him in the way it seemed to affect others. He also said that he had information about experiences that past owners of the property had had.

It seemed interesting, and genuine, so we went to the next stage and sent him the standard questionnaire for residential difficulties. It seemed that there was some psychic talent on his side of the family – his grandfather had been a medium – but no religious affiliations. It also transpired that the information about the past owners had been received after they'd moved in from neighbours, so would fall under the definition of hearsay from our point of view. It was useful background data, but we'd be focusing more on the current problems. What we thought most interesting was his belief that the presence wanted to keep them there rather than drive them away.

More information about the house came to light. Three of the four cellars that had been discovered had been sealed, the other had access to the outside. A friend of the client's whose grandfather had lived in the house had said that he wasn't allowed to go down there but didn't know why. Apparently, it had been used as a dairy and storage area and there had been episodes of taps turning themselves on and off without apparent cause. A previous resident remembered seeing what looked like an old lady standing by the kitchen range, who seemed to be scared of something else. The history of the house was only known as far back as 1901, when it had been built using the walls of a previous structure as the footings.

Communication switched from email to phone at this point, allowing us to get a better sense of the client. He came across as a straight, no-nonsense sort of chap, interested in the welfare of his family. Someone like that is normally an ideal client, since it is helpful to be able to talk directly about a subject. An appointment was set up for us to visit the house to see what we could find. The one caveat that the client made was to insist that his children should know nothing of our work, since he didn't want them to be worried. They had encountered some phenomena in the cellar themselves (cold spots, a profound feeling of discomfort and an inability to stay down there for any length of time), but we felt that as long as the client told us everything we'd be able to work around that. So I travelled down from London to Bristol for a pre-visit meeting and the next day Ian, Jane and myself travelled out to see the client.

One potentially useful detail that came out in conversation

was that one of the children, a pubescent girl, had been getting some very interesting dreams. It seemed that she had been getting a number of messages from her dead grandmother indicating some form of attempt at protection and that this might relate to the ghost of a 'little old lady' that the client's wife had seen by the cooking range, without any feelings of malevolence. If the two were linked, then it was possible that either the ghost by the range was granny, or that it was something else entirely using the granny as a mask through which to communicate with the girl. The family's psychic friend had confirmed that the grandmother was trying to protect the girl as well and the girl had been made aware of it. We left both options open for the time being, deciding that we'd be better able to work out which it was once we'd seen the place for ourselves.

The journey was simple until we got to the edge of the property, where the narrow country lanes were only a few inches wider than the car. We did, however, get a chance to look out from a nearby hill and survey the area around the house with the help of a map. We were definitely getting a sense of something not quite right from the direction of the house, starting some way down the lane. But that was why we were there, so down the lane we went. It was an interesting drive, with steep hills and sharp corners, but eventually we came to the actual drive of the farm and that was when the atmosphere became strong enough to confirm it.

At the end of the drive sat the main farm complex. The house was obviously modern, a white two-storey affair on a concrete base. What looked like a couple of old stable blocks lay beyond it. There was a four-wheel drive outside the house and all the other things one might expect to find in a farmyard. Ian went to ring the bell while Jane and I stretched after the journey. The client answered and I was able to take a good look at him from a distance as greetings were exchanged. He looked as I'd expected from the emails and Ian's briefing, a solid, dependable man who preferred plain dealings and plain language. There was no sense of anything strange attached to him, which was a good start. Jane and I joined the group and we went inside.

The client, his wife, Ian, Jane and I sat around the table to discuss what had been going on. We ran through what had already been covered, probing for more detail. It came out that their eldest son had seen something in the woods behind the house and had a strong feeling that there was a well on the property that had something to do with the cause of the trouble. This was noted and added to the list of things to check when we went outside. But the first thing to do was walk the house. I stayed downstairs with the clients, explaining the process while Ian and Jane went upstairs to take a look. Upstairs, there were several bedrooms and everything seemed to be in order. They returned a few minutes later and after a brief discussion the client headed out to collect their kids from school and take them somewhere to give us time to work.

Next was the cellar. We'd fetched flashlights from the car for this, since we didn't want to take any chances. If the cellar was the centre of activity then this was potentially the risky part. We set things up so that Ian would initially work inside the cellar, with Jane at the foot of the steps maintaining a line of sight with Ian and me at the top minding the door. I was in the rear guard for a change because if the door closed and jammed I was the most likely to be able to reopen it. The flashlights were a precaution in case the lights went out while we had people down there. After a last-minute kit check, Ian went down the stairs, followed by Jane. Ian started to look round the cellar, reporting back in a loud clear voice as he moved round. There was something, but it wasn't anything he could put his finger on. At the same time, I was reassuring the client's wife, explaining what Ian was doing and why we were arranged as we were. We decided that it was worth trying a different arrangement, with Ian and Jane swapping places. She managed to get a little more from the room and a strong feeling that we needed to be looking in the woods behind the house for more information.

The next move then was outside, down a hill by the side of the house and into the woods. As soon as we crossed the tree line, the atmosphere changed. For a start, it was too quiet – the birdsong was muted and sound didn't seem to travel as expected. All three of us were suddenly on edge as we moved further in, to the bottom of the hill and into wet soil. It was muddy in places, but not so bad we couldn't walk. I caught sight of something deeper in, what looked like an old black Transit van parked behind a tree some distance away – the sort of thing where you'd expect to find a couple of MI5 agents and a camera in the back. I drew the others' attention to it and they agreed with me, so we decided it was worth investigating.

As we penetrated further, the ground got more difficult to cross. We carefully picked our way between the trees, maintaining a view of the van. Distance was starting to get a little skewed, too. We can't have gone more than a hundred yards but it felt more like half a mile. We lost sight of the van a couple of times, then saw it again and pressed on. Then suddenly the van disappeared. One second it was there, the next it was gone. Ian moved to higher ground to get a better view of where it had been, but could see nothing. He also realised that there was no way a van could have got into that position in the first place. I tried screwing my eyes up to see anything that could have looked like a van, but without success. It was Jane who voiced the thought running through everybody's mind: 'We've been duped'.

There was a horrible moment then when I thought we might be dealing with fairies. This sort of distraction technique is a classic fey tactic and if we were indeed having to deal with them then everything would be different. One doesn't mess with the fey if it can be avoided – folklore is full of examples about why not – and if we'd walked into a fey vs. human situation then all we could do was hope for a peaceful settlement between the two parties and pray that nobody got hurt in the process. Fortunately, we all felt that this wasn't one of those times. There was no sense of *otherness* and the world around us seemed as real and as local as it should have. Whatever we were dealing with was smart, but it was not a member of the Faerie.

While we felt a little foolish about having fallen for such an old trick, we took it as a good sign that there was definitely something going on. If whatever-it-was was willing to expend so much energy on throwing us off the scent then we were probably getting somewhere. As we headed back, the ground was much harder to cross than it had been on the way out. Undergrowth that had been almost unnoticed before now seemed to snag our boots with every step. It was a hard slog to get back towards the house and seemed to take forever.

As we got to a clearing in the woods, Jane held up her hand: she'd picked something up. Ian and I both scanned the area and found what had set her off, something between two trees that seemed to be watching us. Ian moved uphill to firmer ground and round to the other side of the clearing as I took up position on the near side. Jane moved forward, ready to try talking to it.

As Jane moved into position, Ian and I started to focus ourselves ready to attack in case it decided to try anything funny. It had already tried distraction and hadn't expected us to spot it, so we had to be prepared for another defensive move. All I could see was a rough humanoid outline about the same size and shape as a teenage girl, like a shimmer in the air – but its fear was easy to sense. Jane stepped forward, asking who it was and what was wrong. I couldn't hear its response, but judging from the reactions of the others it wasn't exactly keen on cooperating. Jane tried again without success, and Ian challenged it, saying that if it didn't start answering we'd destroy it without further warning. He signalled me to check I was ready and I responded that I was. I may not have been able to hear it, but I could see where it was and had sufficient psychic energy ready to go that it would have been nothing but a bad memory by the time I was done. Given that Ian was in a similar state, it was obvious that this could be sorted out pretty soon one way or the other. Ian gave the order to make ready and Jane tried to step back to give us a clear field of fire.

She couldn't. The mud had closed around her feet in such a way as to make moving more than an inch impossible. One second her feet were sitting in two boot-sized holes, the next second that mud had closed completely over her feet and was refusing to budge. While irritating, this wasn't the problem the entity might have hoped it was. I still had a clear line of sight and Ian only had to move a couple of paces to get a better angle. Jane's ability to look after herself wasn't a problem either. We all knew her shields would easily absorb whatever splash there was from a hit so finely targeted. Presumably the entity realised that too and finally started to see sense and talk.

Jane started with the simple stuff and moved quickly on to useful information. It turned out that the entity was a water spirit or elemental (classified as an Undine by Paracelsus in the sixteenth century – basically a spiritual personification of the essence of water), lost and panicky. It had been pulled out of the local groundwater via the old well several decades back and ended up in the cellar of the house when it was still in use as a working area (this, of course, tied in with what the eldest son had sensed initially). Since then it had been trying to attract attention to get help with being returned to a natural water source, but had panicked when we arrived and made a break for it. It had, apparently, thought that we were there to destroy it rather than help and had used a great deal of its reserves to get clear of the house for a short time and send us off on a wild-goose chase, hoping we'd get lost or give up and go home. This wasn't necessarily wrong, at least about our intentions, since we were quite prepared to do just that as a last resort and had been only a few seconds from firing when it started to communicate. Jane soothed it somewhat, assuring it that now we knew what was going on, we were going to help rather than take any other course of action. We let it go, since being away from the house was draining it and we now knew what to do to solve the problem. It was time to head back indoors.

The trip back was much easier than the trip out. The ground was firmer, our perception of the terrain clearer. Jane's feet moved easily the moment the entity had left and we were back at the house fairly quickly. One interesting thing about our excursion was that the well seemed nowhere to be found. We'd checked the map and a plan of the farm, but searching the area showed no sign at all. We did find an arch of trees that had been mentioned, but that was all.

Once we'd got back to the house and removed our extremely muddy boots, Jane asked for a glass of water. She needed something to carry the spirit out of the house so it could be released. With that, she and Ian went downstairs to the cellar while I waited by the door. We weren't taking any chances, just in case we'd been misled again. Jane re-emerged shortly afterwards, carrying a now cloudy glass of water. We got our boots back on and went to the back of the house. With a smile, she threw the water out of the glass in an arc through the air and we were treated to the most beautiful rainbow I've ever seen as it fell to earth. Jane turned around, grinning from ear to ear. She'd heard the spirit singing with joy as it was set free and her laugh was infectious for a moment as we went back into the house to tell the client's wife what had happened.

As soon as we went back inside, we noticed the change in atmosphere. The client's wife was looking much happier and far less tired than she had been. We explained the situation to her – what had been causing the problems, and why, and what we'd done about it. While we were confident that the situation had been resolved, we wanted to check the outbuildings just to be sure.

Ian and I headed back out again, while Jane stayed back at the house with the client's wife. We checked the tool shed and found nothing. Then the farm dog came up to investigate what we were up to, so I spent a few seconds fussing her before I realised she was trying to get our attention. She started leading us towards one of the outbuildings and we followed. Once you've seen enough weird things, the idea of a dog leading you somewhere really doesn't phase you – and I'd watched *Lassie* as a kid so the idea wasn't entirely new to me. We started at one end, scanning to see what we could find, moving one stall at a time as the dog followed close behind us, ears flat to the top of her head. This seemed to have been an animal pen at one time or another, but appeared to be currently out of use. There was a cold spot at the end of the passageway where it led into a utility room and we performed a basic space-clearing exercise that seemed to deal with it. The dog was certainly a lot happier. Her ears popped back up and she started wagging her tail. I thanked her for her help with a scratch under the chin and we moved on to the other outbuilding, which read as clear.

The job done, we headed back to the house for a final debrief and to say our goodbyes. Normally we'd have stayed a little longer, but the client wanted to bring the kids home reasonably soon and we wanted to cause as little disruption to them as possible. The client's wife phoned the client, explaining that we were done and making arrangements for us to meet and deal with the details of invoicing and suchlike. Ian and Jane went to meet him, having dropped me off in the nearby village so that I could get cigarettes for the trip home. The last details completed, we set out for home.

And that should have been that.

A couple of days later, however, we had an email from the client. It seemed that their eldest son had visited and reported experiencing the same trouble as he had before when trying to go into the cellar. The client's wife had developed a headache not long after and gone to take a nap, which was somewhat out of character for her. While she was asleep, she heard what she felt was child-like squabbling along the lines of 'Didn't get me', 'Yes, we did!'. They told us that they were going to wait for their psychic friend (the one who'd done the reading all those years ago and who had become a friend of the family) to visit the following week and see what she thought, but would keep us informed in the meantime. We were glad that they'd let us know as quickly as they had, since I was staying in Bristol for a couple of days to catch up with some friends and recharge my batteries a little before heading back to London. Since everyone was in the same place at the same time, it was decided that the best thing to do was move directly to head the problem off and work remotely.

As far as I'm concerned remote working is odd, even by the standards that I'm used to. For me, it works in the same way that some people use astral travel or remote viewing. I'm only able to get anywhere normally if I've been to the target location before, unlike the people who do it more regularly and are able to get to places 'blind'. We settled down into comfortable positions and relaxed, letting our minds slide out of our bodies and back towards the client's house. The first thing I spotted was the farm dog, which had noticed me arriving in the yard. The air was still and everything seemed quiet. I could sense something in the house, although I was still getting my bearings and wanted to be sure of myself before going inside. Ian and Jane were my backup, standing by in case anything went wrong. While the dog was trying to work out what I was, I reset my astral body to resemble that of another dog to make her feel more comfortable. Ian told me later that I looked more like wolf than dog, but it was enough to settle the farm dog down and get her to lead me round the place, sniffing for anything that shouldn't have been there. The outbuildings seemed fine, and this was confirmed by Ian and Jane from their positions. That was good, since it meant that we'd cleared them out with the first sweep and wouldn't need to worry about them any more.

Then it was time to examine the house. I returned to my regular shape and let myself float up to the roof of the house. Since we were expecting trouble to be in the basement, it seemed sensible to start at the top and work my way down. That way if things were spreading I'd hit the edge before the centre and stay out of trouble and we'd have an idea of how bad things were. There's no point being a casualty if one can avoid it, since it just makes extra work for the team and everyone points and laughs at you afterwards.

The attic rooms and top floor were fine and all I was getting from the ground floor was a faint tingle. If there was still something there it wasn't coming across as anything of particular note. Down into the cellar, where there was a slight trace, but nothing specific that could be detected. I stopped and thought for a second, and looked around again. There was a lot of electricity moving around down there, so I tried looking at the way it was moving to see if I could find anything unusual. Success – I could see a weak presence trying to hide in the electrical field of the freezer. The trick here was to be as quiet as I could about it right up to the moment I hit it, since if it realised I'd found it I'd probably have had to spend the rest of the day chasing it through the house wiring. I focused my energy, marked my target point, took a deep breath and hit it as hard as I could, intending to at least stun it long enough to rip it out of the wiring and send it back to wherever it had come from. However, I'd slightly overestimated the thing and as a result had hit it so hard that there was nothing but a small amount of residue left and that was busily evaporating. Fair enough, I thought, this way saves us all a certain amount of effort – not entirely my first choice but, when something's going after people, their needs outweigh the thing's every time.

I had Ian and Jane run another check over the whole farm and we established a shield over the now-cleared, checked and double-checked house to stop anything else getting in there uninvited.

The job done, I withdrew from the target area and headed back home. I slid back into my body, did a few breathing and stretching exercises and went in search of coffee and a cigarette. I was feeling rather drained once again and wanted to get my act together in my own way. While I did this, Ian went into his office to send a report back to the client, explaining what we'd done, what we'd found and how we'd dealt with it. It had been a hard hour's work, but I was glad to have things under control for the client. They'd seemed like decent people and I wanted to do what I could for them.

We heard back from the client that his son had tried to contact us without success and that their psychic friend was unfortunately no longer able to visit and give her opinion. Both the client and his wife reported feeling very tired and anxious over the preceding day or so and that there had been some difficulty with the cellar lights at about the right time for it to be while I was engaging the target. Ian wrote back with a request for as much information as they could give us to help analyse the problem and get as much done for them as possible without the need for them to incur further fees.

It was just under two weeks before we heard back, via an email from the son describing his experiences with the cellar. He reported that on each of his several visits over the two weeks previous to his mail he had felt a presence that was steadily increasing in strength. During his visit that day he'd been unable to go more than two steps down the stairs into the cellar without feeling nauseous and he felt that this oppressive atmosphere was now spreading into the ground floor of the house and draining anyone within reach of energy. He went so far as to estimate that, at this rate of expansion, it would have expanded to fill the whole house in the next few days and be causing what he described as 'serious damage to anyone in the house from that point on'. From his visits earlier that week he was convinced that the entity was still centred on the cellar and was now attempting to drive the family from the house. He also mentioned that they'd been told in the past that the key to removing it was related to a grave near the house and that his feeling was that the grave was linked to the well we'd previously been unable to locate. He'd not been able to locate the well either although he'd seen the same archway in the trees that we had, and had also seen what appeared to be some form of religious ceremony taking place 'at the end of the well nearest the house'. Sadly he was unable to provide any further information about this.

Obviously, we were deeply concerned by this for a number of reasons. The fact that all three of us had scanned the house remotely and found it clean and then shielded it to prevent anything from entering uninvited, meant that there shouldn't have been any activity in the house at all. What concerned us more was that while the well had been discussed earlier, this was the first mention of a grave that we'd heard.

Ian, Jane and I discussed the situation by telephone. It was becoming more likely that we'd need to go back in person and, in view of the client's financial position, we decided to reduce our normal fee by half as a one-off gesture of good faith. It was also decided that we'd continue to scan the house from a distance, upgrade the shielding to a level as near to that used to defend our own homes (which as you might imagine is somewhat more than would normally be required by a client) as was safe for the family, and to ask another member of the Athanor team who had so far had nothing to do with the case to run another scan to make sure we hadn't missed anything. We scanned and it was still clean. We upgraded the shields to a level normally only used by people who piss bad magicians off on a semi-regular basis and got a 'thumbs up' from the external check. At this point, that house was secure enough for me to be happy to use it as a hide-out. We also rearranged our diaries, on the assumption that the client would want to take up our offer and get us there as soon as we could make it. I even had a bag packed and ready to go so I could get to Bristol to join the team as quickly as possible when the call came in.

Just for our own data, we also asked the client if it would be possible for the son to show us where the well was located and for more information about the grave.

Two days later, we got the reply. Apart from tiredness, the only effect noticed by any family member other than the son was the client's wife experiencing a sudden bout of nausea and vomiting that cleared up in a few hours. The client himself had suffered some insomnia and had smelt cooking in the kitchen early in the morning. No other effects were reported beyond a feeling of being watched.

Again, we discussed the situation and the radically different accounts of what was happening and came to the conclusion that the best thing to do was wait until another incident that directly caused them to worry. We thought that the son was reacting to something he expected to be there, which is not uncommon in someone with an untrained psychic talent. We thought this primarily because the experiences he was reporting were so radically different from those of his parents – who had thus far been completely straight with us to the best of our knowledge and had no reason to either exaggerate or downplay what was happening. We were sure that the area was clear, and felt it most likely that the feelings of being watched were due more to stress than anything else. As such, we asked them to let us know if anything else happened and decided to keep the reduced-rate option open to them indefinitely.

I think it's important to emphasise here that we didn't think the son was making his account up. Our position was based on the difference in the two accounts, and the client, who had been our primary point of contact throughout, had not mentioned any of the phenomena the son reported. We made sure that we clearly explained this to the client and encouraged them to keep us abreast of the situation so we could act as circumstances allowed.

So we were a little surprised when the tone of communications changed from the friendly footing we'd previously enjoyed to a considerably more aggressive posture. It started with an email that weekend to Ian from the psychic friend. She intimated that the client and his wife were in fact hysterical about the situation and that she herself had had doubts when we remarked on the ease of the removal of the water spirit. Now, admittedly the actual removal process had been relatively simple – once we'd tracked it, identified it and persuaded it that our intention was to help if possible – because the spirit was eventually willing to cooperate with its removal. I wouldn't be inclined to say that the process itself was an easy one by any means. However, it was the psychic friend's opinion that we 'wouldn't catch this blighter so easily'. She went on to say that the household felt it was in danger (something the client had not said to us at any point) and that someone had to help. She would have done so already, apparently, but it was beyond her capabilities. She finished by effectively ordering us to go back to the house and to reply directly to the client as she would probably be there by then.

Ian emailed the client on Monday morning, asking for clarification on what was happening. We now had a situation where two almost entirely different accounts were being given to us and we needed to understand which was correct. The client's reply was also more aggressive in tone, now saying that the original atmosphere had returned to the house and that the son was offended by our observations. More new information came too, in that the son had checked the cellar after the remote working and found nothing but a few residual cold spots, but now felt that he was under attack the moment he crossed the threshold. He told us that he would forward a copy of an email from the psychic friend, who had his complete confidence and a perfect track record in everything she'd told them.

The email was a recommendation that the client should tell us 'that things are as bad as they're likely to get without there being physical harm done'. She went on to reiterate her opinion that the family was in great danger and recommend that we return to the site in person. Regarding her email to Ian, she said that 'someone had to tell him about his obligations'.

We had, at this point, been ready to revisit the site for a full week. Diaries were being deliberately left open to accommodate them. No such request had been received.

We then received an email directly from the son. This was blunt to the point of rudeness and stated that he was positive that our analysis was wrong, based on the natural gift that had been in his family for generations. He was not anticipating anything because he had sensed 'only a trace of the spirit' after the follow-up. He then asserted that, because we had been paid for an initial visit, we were obligated to complete the work at no further charge and that the entity was now exacting revenge on the family because of the inconvenience we had caused it. He even went so far as to compare us to plumbers who had failed to fix a leaking tap.

At this point, we found ourselves at something of a crossroads. We wanted to find out what was wrong and deal with it. They wanted us to find out what was wrong and deal with it. But it was becoming apparent to us that whatever we did was not going to be good enough and that taking care of things would require firm action.

There was some debate about the best way to deal with

this situation. It was obvious that the client was now somewhat antipathetic to us, as were those around him and we wanted the case closed and whatever might have been troubling them removed with despatch.

We decided to make the client an offer. We would visit the site again, examine the building and deal with whatever we found once, free of charge. However, it came with some conditions. Since it was obvious that we hadn't been told everything, a complete briefing would be required covering everything that had happened before and after our previous visit. We would also require that everyone concerned (including the children) be present, especially the son and the psychic friend, so that they could see for themselves that the job had been done. We also wanted them present so that they could show us the well that the psychic friend felt was so important, but nobody had been able to locate.

We have yet to receive an answer.

I should perhaps explain more clearly why we felt these conditions were necessary. Since the situation had worsened only after people had been coming and going between the house and other places, we had to consider that whatever they felt was still present had been attaching itself to members of the family and travelling off-site with them when we were working. It was certainly the best model we had that would fit the facts, and having everybody present at once would cut that line of escape off. We had to eliminate the son as a possible factor also. It was his insistence that seemed to be keeping the situation tense and we wanted to corroborate his impressions. If he was right, and we were unable to pick up what he could, then he would have been able to assist us in finding whatever it was still causing difficulties and eliminating it.

It seemed to us that without this level of cooperation we

would be unable to do any more for them. In fact, we were only willing to go as far as we did, with a lot of off-site work, discussion, remote sensing and such, because of the children involved. We wanted to sort this out for the clients, of course, and our pride makes us unwilling to walk away from something we've started, but without cooperation we were unable to proceed any farther. Despite our best efforts to make this clear to the client, we didn't receive that cooperation and our hands were tied.

Looking back on the case over a year later, I still regret that we were not able to close it properly. But I've included it in this book as an example of how we work in partnership with a client, how communication needs to flow both ways and why we ask so many questions before we start working directly on the problem. It also demonstrates why cooperation is important to finding a solution. You will have noticed in chapter ten that the client felt able to tell us everything as quickly as she could, and that, although the husband was absent, we were given free rein to act and talk to whoever we felt we had to. That was not the case here, and I feel that if any one factor is responsible for our inability to end the problems at the farm then that was it.

chapter twelve

TWENTY-FOUR HOURS IN MONMOUTH

Everybody loves a haunted pub, except the people who live and work in them. I'd had an SMS from a friend of mine called Nick who's a witch and has been a friend for a few years, and a witch for many more. We'd been drunk together quite a few times and worked together before when he needed an extra body, so I know I can trust his opinions and the way he works. What he sent me was this: 'You up for a spot of ghostbusting?'

My interest, as you might expect, was aroused. As a rule I don't get text messages like this, even from witches. So a brief phone conversation ensued as he told me about a friend who knew someone who had a pub and the pub was having trouble. Nick had been asked if he'd mind having a look and his first reaction was to call me and see if I'd like to go along too.

My early researches were surprisingly unproductive. I had trouble finding any data on the internet at all. I could see that it was there, but nothing about it. Interesting. But not indicative of anything in particular. We compared diaries and came up with a date – late June 2005. Between setting the date and actually visiting the site I was approached about writing this book. Since I knew I was going to be writing the episode up for the book rather than just for my usual notes, I was able to ask the people involved if they'd be willing to contribute their own points of view on what happened. Hence there will be parts of this chapter that come from people unused to the range of phenomena that I am – as well as (hopefully) a view of my work from someone who's never seen it before.

I travelled down from London to Bristol on the Friday, stayed over with Ian that night, and Nick and I headed over the bridge into Wales the next morning, with the windows down, punk music loud on the stereo and a generally good feeling in our hearts. As we crossed into Wales I made a point of sticking the psychic equivalent of my battle standard on top of the car so I was clearly identifiable and both Nick and myself got a huge rush that had us grinning and laughing our heads off. It looked like someone was on our side for a start!

We'd agreed that, without the pre-visit questionnaires and all the usual paraphernalia that precede an Athanor visit, we'd meet the people involved away from the pub itself. We'd been told that the trouble had escalated dramatically over the week between the summer solstice and our visit and the request for us to have a look had become a flat cry for help or, as Nick put it, 'A nose around has been replaced with kick some serious butt'.

So, a sunny Saturday lunchtime in June found us at a pub called The Anchor directly outside Tintern Abbey. I'm not sure who picked it as the rendezvous, but it was perfect – not too busy at that time of day and 20 minutes by car from Monmouth and the pub we'd been called in to deal with. It's a nice country pub that gives the impression of having been there for years and had a welcoming kind of vibe to it from the moment we saw it. We grabbed a drink and settled in to wait.

We'd arrived first to get a sense of the place and to be able to watch people arrive. Under the circumstances I felt it was important that we gathered as much data as possible, especially before anyone got used to my presence or had time to marshal or hide their feelings.

The first people to arrive were Jaine and Tim, who had first got hold of Nick to tell him what was happening and ask for his help. I'd met Jaine a couple of times before so we had the usual round of saying how great the other looked as she accused me of losing weight and such. Jaine's a reiki healer among other things, so I knew that I could trust her opinions on the energy currents in the target area. I'd not met Tim before, but he seemed to be keeping his head together and seemed very interested in what Nick and I had to say about what was going on. It was good to be able to put them at ease this way – especially before Niki and Baz (the landlady of the pub and her boyfriend) arrived. This way when they got to us they'd have a warm, friendly environment to help them feel safe to talk about what was happening to them.

And, boy, did they need it. Niki was only aware of Nick being there – and had been concerned enough about coming to see him. If she'd known about my presence in advance, she freely admitted she would not have been able to leave the pub to come and see us. This isn't uncommon – one of the things some presences can do to defend themselves is plant the idea that everything's fine and that there's no need to call people in, or that the person coming to help is a bad sort who will steal all your money, burn down the house and run off to marry your dog. It's perfectly normal, so I wasn't surprised and knew that I should handle Niki gently and carefully. I switched down to my quiet, reassuring voice. Again, it was one of those occasions where being large and mildly imposing worked against me as well as for me, although for once I'd be inclined to say that having several earrings and a bald head helped.

I suggested that we started with Niki's account of what had

been happening, followed by Baz, then Tim – who had been dealing with what seemed to be the onset of some psychic talent himself – and finally Jaine. Niki found she couldn't actually talk about it with Baz there, so he left her to talk for a moment as she steeled herself to tell the tale. Niki had been working at The Griffin for the last six years – in that time she'd seen evidence of RSPK (*see* chapter four), including having things thrown at her. In the last year she'd taken charge of the place and that's when things had started to get more interesting. It had started with a bad atmosphere, a sense of things not being right. Niki had a feeling of heaviness, of being cold irrespective of actual conditions. Then the physical effects had really started: her hair was pulled, she could hear voices, there were times when she could see what seemed to be people on the edge of her peripheral vision, and there were episodes of 'sleep paralysis' – a feeling of being held down in bed, unable to move.

She was scared. Things were starting to really get to her. So she called a medium and asked her to come and have a look at the place and see if she could help. The medium came, had a look at the place and said it was out of her league and turned her down flat.

So Niki called for help again. This time, a locally based team of seven 'Ghost-busters' came to visit. This group were willing to take the job on, and managed some form of communication with what was there. While this was taking place, Niki experienced panic attacks and violent feelings of nausea. Sadly, though, it seems that this group were unable to shift things either because, after a short period of relief, things kicked off again and Niki found herself drinking more, as well as having periods of aggressive behaviour that she couldn't remember afterwards.

It was not long after this that a party was held in the flat above the pub. While it was a party in all the usual ways, the photographs that came back from developing showed some interesting effects. In one, a face was evident on the wall, which Niki and the others described as 'wolf-like', and in another a dark, hooded figure could be seen standing next to a window. Interestingly, Niki found herself unable to enter that room and had a strong sense that the hooded figure was unable to cross the threshold either and had to enter and leave the room vertically instead. Sadly, the photos weren't available for us to examine.

The third attempt to get things fixed was with another medium, this time from Manchester. The defence this time was even more aggressive. Niki was sick, everybody had a strong taste of blood in his or her mouth and the smell of raw sewage filled the air. Fortunately, it seems that this medium was pretty damned good at her job because she was able to come back with some good data.

The first information related to the kitchen. Sue (the medium) was pretty sure that people had been poisoned there and the spirit of a small child named Emily had been seen. This may well have related to the history of the pub, since it had apparently been an orphanage at one time. There were also indications of a puritan-like figure. Sue estimated that there were in excess of twenty separate presences within the pub and flagged the cellar as a point of particular interest, predicting that seven of those presences would be removed from there. Sadly, though, it seemed that she wasn't able to shift them. Nonetheless, it was the best data we had, and would turn out to be very useful.

After this, a child staying on the premises saw clear shapes and figures in the shadows and specifically a large black dog roughly the size and shape of a Rottweiler with glowing green eyes that seemed to be watching everything that was happening around it. This caused the child a fair amount of disquiet such that it was unwilling to stay on the premises.

At Christmas in 2004, Niki arranged to have the pub blessed by two priests, one of whom ran the parish church directly across the road. Things seemed to calm down significantly after this as they worked their way through the place systematically, blessing each room and corridor individually. The only place they missed out was the attic. Things calmed down. Life started to return to normal and everything seemed right with the world.

Life went on like this for a few months and then a new member of staff joined the team to work behind the bar. All the old effects came back – unreasonable rages forgotten when they passed and physical illness in several members of staff. Niki even started to get urges to harm herself by scratching her face over and over again. Fortunately, she was able to resist those urges, but it wasn't easy for her to do so. The new member of staff didn't last long.

Things were obviously getting worse. Each reactivation was stronger and nastier than the one before it. Niki was quite understandably terrified and it was really starting to wear her down and make her ill. The situation was getting her to such a state where she didn't want to sleep in the pub if she could avoid it. She'd asked the head barmaid to move into the flat and oddly enough nothing had happened to her at all. She just wasn't getting anything. While interesting, this wasn't something that concerned me. Stuff just doesn't happen to some people and I have no idea why.

Baz now returned and was able to fill in a few details of atmosphere and suchlike that corroborated what we'd already been told as well as helping Niki keep a grip on the situation. Although, once I'd reassured her and persuaded her to start talking, she'd been able to keep going, the mere act of telling somebody about what had happened to her was obviously distressing. I frequently find myself admiring the courage of the people I help when they tell me about these things. I realise that it can't be easy to say such things to strangers and taking that first step of trusting someone with information that may well not even be known to close friends is a leap of faith.

Tim was next. Tim had been taking dictation, in what seemed to me to be medieval French. He produced two pages of typed-up notes (with rough translations that he wasn't entirely sure about) for Nick and myself to take a look at. Unsurprisingly, he told us that he had no knowledge of medieval French, but went on to say that he had no modern French or Latin either. The running themes seemed to be fear and spirits,[2] and there was a distinct feeling of wrongness about the paper as well.

Tim has been kind enough to make a few notes of his own about the case, so I'm including them here to give an idea of what it's like to have this sort of thing happen to you. I'll be quoting him as I go along, but let's start with his views on what had happened before Nick and I were called in.

> I moved back to Monmouth in March 2004. I first noticed something strange in The Griffin late one night around May/June 2004. Standing in the doorway/steps area (by the toilets) was a Puritan/Wesleyan type character, very tall, beard/moustache and very, very nasty looking. Beside him

2 Under normal circumstances I don't exactly have a good grasp of medieval French either, but I know enough French and Latin to be able to pick out the themes from this. There was no way I was going to stop and find the reference material I'd need for a full translation, either, since it won't surprise you to learn that I was starting to get a bad feeling about this whole affair. It was certainly far more serious than the initial information had led me to understand.

was a little blonde girl looking very scared. I wrote a note to Niki asking how old the pub was. She looked horrified at my question and, when I told her what I had seen, she got rather upset. It was then that I discovered my spiritual side and learnt that different spiritual people see and feel different things.

Niki told me about happenings like glasses hurtling across the bar, shadows moving around the walls and feeling 'the chills'. She invited me upstairs to wander the rooms and I was instantly aware of many different spirits and a feeling of pressure on top of me.

I was invited by Niki to join a group of her friends, one of whom was a High Priestess and five others, all female friends on different levels of spiritual awareness. They decided to get a group of 'clearers' into the pub but much to my displeasure excluded me. I did not feel at all comfortable watching them move around the pub in a large group and thought they didn't know what they were doing. They used a lot of black and negative energies to assist them and it became obvious over the coming months that they had actually made things worse. Many people noticed Niki's character changing drastically and more occurrences of banging, stomping and movement of shadows.

A birthday party was held, which on the whole was a good night. However, the birthday photos taken on a digital camera showed two faces about six or seven feet up the chimney breast. These two heads looked as if they had been on fire and were like a cross between a man and dog's skull. Many people studied the pictures and agreed that the heads could not merely be light, marks on the wall or shadows. Also, some photos had been taken in various rooms in the pub, many showing orbs and coloured spheres, and a few with shadows. The most significant photo had been placed on a few PCs but **no one could print off or re-edit the photos.** Although I experienced great difficulty getting a print off, eventually I was able to highlight various areas of the photo and in the top room window overlooking the church was a figure that can only be described as the emperor Palpatine out of *Star Wars*. A dark, cloaked figure with a crooked staff and curved scarab knife with piercing red eyes could be seen as a reflection behind the photographer. I saw this figure many times in the pub and it was agreed that no one was to enter the top room although I insisted nothing would hurt me if I went in there. In fact, I did and told whatever it was to leave Niki alone.

Members of staff who stayed at the pub underwent personality changes and bouts of extreme happiness and instant sadness combined with aggression that was never brought on by provocation. Niki had started drinking more. I felt that this was poisoning her and one of her spiritual friends agreed. Niki felt the pub was also affecting her son and her own happiness. Over several months many of us involved in the small spiritual group experienced a metallic taste in the mouth, similar to sucking a teaspoon or having a mouthful of blood mixed with excess saliva.

Niki began to show more symptoms of a split personality but felt safe in my company and I stayed with her a few nights in a protective role. Another so-called expert was called in to exorcise the place. This time I was to be involved as it was revealed I had a Templar connection and the area was thought to be an old Templar haunt.

On the morning of their visit we realized that there were no candles in the pub and I went to fetch some. On my return, the main character in the clearing of the pub, whom we shall call Julie, said that many people had been poisoned in the kitchen area. Over the course of about four hours I believe that we were each in turn channelled, with some laughing quite eerily and others, even those not channelled but merely attending the premises, feeling immense sadness and uncontrollable bouts of crying.

When it was revealed I was the one with the Templar ancestry Julie wanted to sit me down and channel me. I was asked to pick a number and replied 'seven' and this was the number of spirits she believed I could assist in removing from the cellar area. I was told I was providing an immense amount of energy and was being drained.

Many of the people present vomited but afterwards things were OK for a while. However, soon it was business as usual with Niki showing signs of a split personality and both of us sensing the return of many things evil. The taste in our mouths returned and the rest of the spiritual group refused to have anything to do with us. Niki and I had a bizarre falling out over nothing and up to Christmas that year (2004), when two Church of England vicars visited the pub, blessed every room and blessed each of us, we very rarely spoke.

Christmas came and went but we soon realized things were still not right. It was around March that I met Jaine through a mutual friend working at The Griffin. It was obvious she was very deep and spiritual and wanted to help. She suggested that what The Griffin needed was a visit from Dave Devereux and her cousin Nick the High Priest. I was concerned for Niki as I thought the pub wanted or needed HER. Several times she had made the weirdest noise in her throat, a sound I can only describe as someone being murdered shouting for help. I had been experiencing a lot of ringing in the ears, whispers of Latin and French and also seen Niki in states of confusion about who was telling her the truth.

The first Latin 'message' I received was in a dream in about February 2005 in which three men in suits called at my door and said they needed my spiritual help. They drove me far into the countryside up a hill to a narrow lane with stone walls on either side. We stopped near a hill on the right with trees on the top. On getting out of the car I noticed the words 'De Seras Templar' on the boot of the car. I was told I was preventing progress and was getting too near to the truth. They then set about me with knives that I can only describe as triangular with a central circular hole. The other Latin/French messages came while I was with Nick and Jaine watching *Finding Nemo*, and more came when I was at home, or at The Griffin, The Nags Head or at work in St Weonards, which is about three miles from Garway.

I was also able to tell Niki that one of the pub's regular customers was a Gatekeeper and that the fireplace was a Gateway. This came as softly whispered words in my ear while I was sitting in the pub.

Meanwhile, Niki had found a new partner who I believe was beneficial to her and right for her spiritually. His name was Baz, a gentle giant who, we discovered, also had a sense of what was happening and indeed had experienced many sleepless nights with Niki at the pub. I arranged with Jaine to have Nick and Dave meet us in Tintern.

Jaine had been worrying about me and the time I was spending in The Griffin although I felt that I was helping to protect Niki and Baz. Several times they had called me and said that the atmosphere was awful and I had, whenever I could, gone over to The Griffin and invited them back to the safety of my flat after sensing that things definitely were not 'right' there. I had seen the Master's dog, felt the pressure bearing down on me and sensed my own mood changes, but in the main had felt strong enough to help. However, I knew I couldn't fix things there so I contacted Dave and Nick.

After briefly explaining the situation I made arrangements to meet them in Tintern in a pub adjacent to Tintern Abbey. I admit that I told Niki and Baz that it was just an initial meeting, although I knew that we would be visiting The

Griffin at some stage that day. It was important to get Niki and Baz to meet Nick to get the benefit of his experience.

When we entered the pub I actually noticed Dave before Nick. I gathered immediately that he was very well-educated, meant business and thought a great deal before opening his mouth. I was pleased to see them both but was a little concerned about how Niki might receive Dave as he looked as though he 'meant business'.

Baz and Niki arrived in the car park and I went out to meet them. Niki was very nervous and I helped to reassure her by telling her that she could sit next to me and that she only had to talk about and do what she felt was comfortable for her. At one point she asked Baz to take a stroll while she explained some of the events. I think that she felt that airing these events might put Baz off being in the pub or around her though I felt that he wasn't stupid and, because he cared so much for her, he was willing to do anything he could to alleviate the situation.

I reassured Niki throughout the ensuing conversation, trying to get her to open up. This she found difficult because the pub was affecting her mentally and physically and also, she felt, affecting her child and her relationship with Baz.

I helped Niki explain some of the events and indeed had brought a notebook with some things that Niki didn't even know about, instances of her shouting and changing character, my ancestry with Martyrs and Masons (Templars) and the feelings I had experienced throughout the time I had known Niki and of course the various so-called 'experts' who had said they could resolve the happenings and atmosphere.

We asked a few more questions to help us be sure we had an overall picture of what was going on, then I suggested it was time to head out into the car park, so I could check each person over for any external influences and make sure they were properly shielded for what was to come. Niki found a corner of the car park and tried to make herself small while I worked on the other three. Nothing psychically odd, but she was cringing into a corner as though she hoped we might forget all about her. There were distinct remnants of external interference on two of them, so I got that cleared off and shielded each individually myself, as supplements to their own natural defences. I'd already decided that we weren't going to be taking any chances and Nick seemed to agree as he stood back and monitored my work to make sure I hadn't missed anything.

Getting Niki through this phase was starting to look tricky. Up until now I'd been playing it very relaxed, easy to talk to and humorous – but it looked like time to shift gears a little. She was standing in the corner of the car park as she had been when I started and would have turned invisible given half a chance. Catching her eye as she looked round to check what I was doing, I locked her gaze and beckoned her forward. Slowly, as though each step was a battle inside her, she started to move towards me. After a few steps she was in an area with sufficient room for me to start work. Keeping her gaze, I approached her. 'Niki,' I said, keeping my voice low, 'We're going to fix this, but you need to trust me. This is what I do and everything that's been bothering you will end today. Will you trust me to do that?' She nodded slightly, obviously still terrified. I scanned and cleared her as quickly as I could, locking the shields down so there was no way anything else could start influencing her. She started to look a little better, but still ill. It was obvious that whatever was waiting for us back at the pub had affected her quite profoundly.

Tim again:

> We were, each in turn, asked to stand in front of Dave about fifteen to twenty feet from him, facing him. He placed protection upon us, in Niki's case removing what I thought to be an arrow from her (I could be wrong). When it came to my turn, he stared at me and almost, I felt, straight into me and started to circle me. I tried to be as open and honest as possible and also tried to let him know that I wasn't afraid of what was going to happen. He finished his circuit, appeared to check my aura and said, 'Good enough for me, let's go!' This filled me with a mass of energy and confidence.

With that done, it was time to get in our respective conveyances and start the twenty-mile journey to Monmouth. Time was a-wasting and I needed to talk to Nick.

It turned out to be a short conversation. While it's not uncommon for people to have trouble talking about these things in situ, it was obvious that what was happening at The Griffin was far worse than we'd considered likely. I got the impression that Nick was very happy when I outlined my suggested plan to him, as was Ian in Bristol when he heard it.

The name of the game, ladies and gentlemen, was 'Scorched Earth'.

Given that this place had already successfully resisted attempts at negotiation, communication and pacification, my intentions toward it had become somewhat less than subtle. It was obvious to me that nothing short of gross psychic violence would have a chance of doing the job so we spent the rest of the journey getting ourselves together and preparing for what was going to be a gruelling process. We weren't going to a séance, we weren't going to investigate – we were going to walk into that building, hunt down every single psychic, spiritual, trans-dimensional and any other non-physical presence and kill it by whatever means were necessary.

This place had caused so much pain, suffering and general unpleasantness that there was no way I was leaving until the job was done, no matter how long that took.

As we came to within half a mile of the pub, I generated a shield to help keep the general area stable while we were working, just in case something went wrong at the pub. Then we parked up and made our way to The Griffin, keeping our wits carefully about us for anything unusual. It was a sunny day in Monmouth and busy in the way that only market towns can be on a Saturday afternoon. A short stroll through the busy streets took us toward our target and a rendezvous with the rest of the group.

> Jaine and I [Tim] met Baz and Niki outside the pub and waited for Nick to call us on Jaine's mobile. We were told that they were on their way up town and Jaine and I went to meet them. I remember gazing a long way down the street, a good three-quarters of the length of the main street in Monmouth and I spotted them. All dressed in black with large flowing black coats, hats of character and a purpose about their walk, they seemed to part the oncoming pedestrians like Moses parted the Red Sea. I thought, 'Bloody Hell, they look ominous.'
>
> I felt part of the 'team' walking up town. Dave sensed we were approaching the pub some 50ft from our destination and said so. Photographs were taken and, when Baz and Niki reappeared, we entered the pub with attitude and conviction in speaking to any customers or staff.

It has been said by innumerable people, quite rightly, that first impressions count. Our entrance was specifically calculated to tell all and sundry, physical and otherwise, who was in charge – in through the front door and straight up to the flat. The first room we came to was the kitchen and that seemed as good a place as any for us to set up base camp. I purged the room hard, just driving anything nasty out and shielding the room so it wasn't coming back to interrupt us. With that done it was time to start setting things up. Nick had witchy things to do and I felt that it was time to call in assistance myself. Since the place was right opposite a graveyard, calling in a little backup from the dead seemed like a good idea. Sending Niki off to the bar for a glass of cheap and nasty white rum (or the nearest that could be found in a quality establishment), I opened my kit bag and started unpacking. Since I was working with a ritualist (even a lighter than average one like Nick), I'd decided to bring a lot more physical kit than usual. I'd packed a large black-handled knife, my beloved Tibetan purba and an interesting piece of kit called a Zozo gun, that helps one focus energy in a slightly different way and can come in very handy for a wide variety of nasties. Nick, meanwhile, was setting up his altar on the other counter and getting his own kit ready to go. Niki returned with my drink, and I split it with the dead: half down my neck and half into the air (over the sink to save mess).

Tim's view again:

> Upstairs we were shown, in rather a laid-back manner, how to make Holy Water by Nick. He was obviously ready to get his teeth into the whole affair with malice aforethought! Dave was much more matter of fact. He downed his 'white rum' and proceeded to spit half of it down the sink to ask for assistance from a spirit he regularly worked with.
>
> Dave stayed in contact with his 'team' in London via mobile phone. Nick appeared to be the locator and describer of the spirits and beings while Dave seemed to play more the destroyer. Jaine and myself also played a locating role and this seemed to work well as we each sense different things.

I was mostly concerned for Niki, in case anything tried to have a go at her, but also I didn't want to miss anything. Not a movement, change in temperature or a sound. Dave introduced us to his gun, a splendid looking six-shooter, and this seemed to complement Nick's sword, which again told me that these guys knew what they were doing and were going to kick some evil butts.

At one point I felt I was being attacked and the whole left side of my ribcage felt as if someone had stuffed their fingers in between the ribs and was pulling at my lungs. Dave to the rescue! Producing a white crystal object from his pocket he said, 'Now this might sting a little bit'. He wasn't wrong, I thought I'd been stabbed for about two seconds! Thankfully, the feeling immediately subsided.

Tim's episode was a last-minute attempt to distract us, but not a terribly effective one. I cracked out the last item of preparatory gear – two self-heating cups of guarana-laced espresso with about a ton of sugar: one each. I find I work better when my heart rate's somewhere up in the stratosphere and the usual biofeedback technique I use was only getting me to the point just before dangerously high. I wanted to be sure I was rolling at full speed, so a little help was welcome.

I checked in with Ian in Bristol, letting him know that we were about to get on with it. He was our top cover for the job, watching our backs and throwing in extra energy and zaps where required. It was a little odd not having him by my side for a job, but I was glad to have him at my back.

Finally, the preparations were over. We'd done everything we could to help things go as smoothly as possible. I looked at Nick and raised an eyebrow. Nick looked back at me and grinned in a way that made me very glad he was on my side. I nodded and turned toward the door with Nick behind me.

I took a deep breath and gave the best battle cry I could think of at the time: 'All right, fuckbag, here we come!'

Along the hallway and up the stairs to the top floor first with Nick roaring something Welsh behind me – it felt more like a tiger hunt or charge into battle than a regular job, but I was feeling good about the whole thing so wasn't about to sweat it. We'd left everybody else in the kitchen with orders to stay put until told otherwise. I had a plan in mind and Nick seemed happy enough to let me lead. We started with a sequential hit on each of the four rooms on that floor – two staff rooms, a bathroom and a storeroom. There was also a cupboard to be considered.

We got the first two rooms easily enough – nothing more than background ickyness. Next we took the bathroom and finally the storeroom. This was the room where a number of people had seen figures and the atmosphere had a distinctly unpleasant edge to it. I looked at Nick, he looked at me, and we hit the room hard, catching something I couldn't quite make out that kept shifting position, like a rat hiding behind a skirting board. It was enough to temporarily clear the air and we threw a shield between us and the floor below to stop anything else coming up.

Next was the attic. We'd been told that a previous group had identified something up there, so we wanted to be sure we got it early in the process. I'd cleared and secured the floor below to make sure that if it started moving it wouldn't be able to get very far. Nick clambered up through the hatch in the ceiling and waited for the screams.

He shouted down that he had a contact – something that seemed to be a blue-black sphere with a purple corona. Something *smart*. We'd been half-expecting this, so Nick pushed it to the end of the attic over the bathroom, and I moved into position below ready to hit it hard. On the count,

Nick pushed it straight down to me and I hit it as hard as I could. It took three shots to finally break the thing up to a point where it stopped functioning – three hard shots, two standard bare-handed magic and one with the Zozo gun. This thing was tough. With it dead, we were able to compare notes a little more openly. Our best guess was that this was a primary locus and had directed a lot of the activity happening in the pub. That was why we'd wanted to get up there and hit it first before it had a chance to realise how serious we were about knocking it out and decided to fight back. This was especially important as it was obviously going to try to distract us by trying to harm the others and we certainly weren't going to allow that.

We went over the top floor again, having checked in with Ian to see what he was getting from range. He was the first to pick up on the small cupboard next to the bathroom that we'd previously thought clear. Sure enough, we could pick up on what was in there now – my guess is that the thing in the attic was deliberately hiding it from us. What we had was... Well, if we assign roles for a second the thing in the attic was daddy and this thing was mum. Somewhere between a spider and a queen bee, this looked to be the source of the actual infestation, pumping out little nasties to roam around the building causing trouble for all concerned. Happily, though, it appeared to be locked in place so Nick and I hit at the same time while Ian threw in extra power from his end – straight magical attacks from three directions at once. That seemed to do the trick, so after one last quick scan we decided to move down to the first floor.

Notice I use the word *seemed*. That cupboard was going to be trouble.

However, we didn't know that at the time, so we chased back down the stairs and hit the first floor with some gusto.

Turning right and down the passageway took us to the large living room over the front door of the pub. It was a sunny day outside, but there was a distinct aspect of gloom to the space that didn't quite fit the lighting. Actually, there was a distinct gloom about the whole place, but it really didn't hit me until then. It was a large room with plenty of windows and should have been flooded with light but it was downright dingy. Still, this is not an uncommon thing when dealing with paranormal troubles so it didn't strike me as odd, just sad. The atmosphere in here wasn't great either. It was obvious that this was where people spent a fair amount of time and the general malaise had settled here badly as a result. We hit the room with a general blast of energy to clear it out, then started looking for specific troubles. There were a few minor things that were easily taken care of, but nothing more interesting than that. After the trouble we'd had upstairs, this was a welcome relief and we took a second to catch our breath before moving on.

The next room was a bedroom – it had been Niki's, but she'd decided to live away from the pub because of what was happening, so the room was now unused. As I walked in, I could see immediately why she'd made that choice – I know I wouldn't have wanted to sleep there while it was in that state. The atmosphere was as oppressive here as it had been in the spare room upstairs, certainly not conducive to any form of rest. In the far left-hand corner of the room, beyond the bed, was an opening through to an en-suite bathroom and I really didn't like the impression I was getting from there. In fact, the more I was seeing of this place the less I liked it. I'm used to seeing places that have troublesome areas, but this was more a case of the whole building being wrong. It wasn't good at all and I could see that this was going to be harder work than I'd thought.

We had no choice but to hit the room hard, just like every other room so far. I was becoming very glad that I'd thought to pack the coffee, let alone persuaded Ian to back me up from range. There was nothing specific in this room, just a sense of despair, loneliness and pain. That at least was a bonus. We put a shield over the doorway to the bathroom and focused our energies on cracking the miasma in the bedroom. Solid focus and deep, controlled breathing: sucking the crud in, filtering it through ourselves and breathing the better air out again. A few minutes' work and I could have killed for a smudge stick to do it for me. While they've been part of Ian's standard field kit for years and they're now part of mine, up to this point I'd never felt the need to use one myself. But I don't get to schedule my learning experiences any more than the rest of the world, so I made a mental note at the time and got on with hoovering the crap up with my lungs.

One advantage to doing things this way is the chance to get a really good impression of the area in which you're working. It was becoming obvious to me that The Griffin had been badly troubled for quite a while. The upper floors of the pub were soaked in sadness, anger and almost every other negative emotion you can think of. It would have been getting me down, too, if I didn't have my mind on the job. How anybody could have lived in this environment for any length of time was beyond me and it certainly explained the trouble that Niki had been having. Since she'd been sleeping in this room, the cumulative effect on her would have been enough to explain the personality changes that her friends had noticed.

We moved into the bathroom and the first thing I noticed was the smell. It was obviously clean, but the odour of damp and decay in here was unpleasant and the air was thick and heavy. Scanning the room, Nick and I both picked up something in the shower cubicle. A nod passed between us and we hit it with a punch that should have shattered it on the spot. No effect. A second, and a third that finally knocked it off-balance enough to let the next hit break it apart. Something in the toilet next, hiding in the bowl. Inside the bloody toilet bowl of all places! This was getting ridiculous. An easy kill, though: one shot did the job.

Suddenly, I had the feeling that something was watching me. I looked at Nick and he was obviously getting the same impression. He looked up and I followed his gaze to the ventilation duct in the ceiling. Good spot, I thought, the place knows it's under attack but lacks the brains to do anything about it. The bits we hadn't got to yet were trying to organise themselves to respond, but were so used to getting instructions that they had no initiative. Just as well, really. If everything we were finding had got together and hit us back we'd have been in trouble. We'd probably have to regroup and come back with more people and then it would have been ready for us. As it was, taking the brain out early – before we'd been recognised as a credible threat – had saved us an immense amount of grief. On the count of three we both took a shot at the vent, but our observer managed to get out of the way. It seemed that the best way to deal with this was from another angle, so I called Ian and explained the situation to him. We'd decided to keep him basically in reserve to help with the difficult stuff so that if Nick and I got tired we'd be able to spend a couple of minutes getting ourselves back together while Ian covered our backs. This was when the policy paid off. Nick and I retreated to the bedroom and then Ian hit the bathroom remotely. As artillery barrages go, it was a good one – when we walked back in there wasn't a thing left but the atmosphere itself. That was a simple thing to deal with, but I really didn't want to do too much deep breathing in there. I spoke to Ian again and we flooded the place with enough positive energy to flush the crud out of the air. The change was immediate and obvious: the room got noticeably lighter, and the smell was now a faint whiff in the background. Job done.

We headed back to the kitchen, where the others were waiting for us. I needed a coffee.

Nick and I explained what we'd done and what we'd found as we got some much-needed sugar, caffeine and fluids down our necks. The next stage was to get a barometer reading and we asked Jaine to come with us to see what she thought of the areas we'd been through. Jaine's a reiki practitioner, so has a good sensitivity to energy, and we thought she'd be a good choice to play canary for us.

By the time we got back upstairs to the landing the spider-mommy was back in residence and unimpressed. Obviously the little bugger was able to shift in and out somehow and was avoiding our attempts to kill it that way. Jaine didn't seem particularly happy about this and neither were we. We hit it again, just to keep it busy if anything, and went around the other rooms on the floor. The only problem spot was the storeroom, so Nick and I hit the area with as much energy as we could and moved back downstairs to check the first floor. The priority at this point wasn't to kill anything: we wanted to know where to concentrate on the next sweep and make sure nobody else got hurt in the process. I tend to draw a line between combatants and civilians in these cases and if we need a civilian in a work area they're in and out as quickly as possible with the best protection we can give them. The first floor seemed OK, although there was a fair amount of residual unpleasantness where we'd blasted everything in sight, so we delivered Jaine back to the kitchen and explained how things were going. Niki was looking frightened, Baz was being strong and Tim seemed mainly fascinated by what was going on.

At this point something thoroughly unexpected happened. Nick noticed something spectral and apparently rat-shaped sitting on a beam by my head looking at me with friendly curiosity. This really shouldn't have been there, since we'd cleared the area and shielded it when we first got there. I played it cool, killing it before it had a chance to realise what I intended, but the message was plain. If we didn't do this job right, it wouldn't have been worth the effort. A quick check of my watch on the way up the stairs told me we'd been at it for over two hours already.

I coordinated another three-point attack on spider-mommy in the cupboard, trying to guess when she would phase back in to a state when we could hit her. Nick, Ian and I hit the cupboard in a seemingly random sequence until she showed herself and we were able to hit her all at once. The ploy worked. In one of the gaps between shots she slid back into view just as Nick was about to fire. Ian came in straight away from his end and I had the Zozo gun out of its holster and was firing before I even knew I'd done it. This time we saw her breaking apart rather than disappearing and we kept the fire up on the fragments until they were thoroughly shattered. Since I didn't want to take any chances and I was pissed off that she'd made us look foolish, I hit the cupboard over and over again, sterilising it so that there was no way anything else would want to move in for a long time.

Next was the storeroom. Something was definitely still in here and I was noticing that almost everything we could sense in the building was mobile, skittering like rats or insects behind the skirting boards. Our advantage was that, by taking out the brain in the attic first, the skittering was nothing more than a survival reflex, trying to escape being blasted out of this plane once and for all. Once we'd got the last remnants of the infestation out, we'd be able to deal with any remaining ambient effects in the rooms and lock the place down to stop it happening again.

But the remnants had to go, so we were effectively down to target shooting again, waiting for something to show itself and then hitting it hard. After a while, we felt that we'd got everything and went to get the others.

I felt it was important that Niki especially saw the results of our work while we were still there. We walked her round the ground floor first and she could feel a distinct difference to the place although there was still some residue from our earlier efforts. We explained this and started opening windows to let the warm summer breeze pass through the building. The residue started clearing immediately, like smoke in the wind, and the rooms became lighter – only a little, but noticeably so. We headed up to the second floor.

There was *still* something in the storeroom! It was alone, but scampering around in an area that should have been empty. This didn't make any of us very happy, but shook Niki especially. I had everyone step out of the room, leaving me alone, and had Nick shield the room to stop my quarry from escaping into another part of the building. We already had shields locking off each floor individually, so it wasn't going up or down, but this would make sure it stayed in the room with me, where I'd be able to get at it. Remembering the story of a rat-catcher I'd read somewhere, I stood in the middle of the room silently. I let my senses open up completely, feeling it move to and fro looking for a way out. Keeping still, being as passive as possible as though I wasn't even there, I watched as it tried to find a chink in Nick's shield and failed. I was banking on it being stupid and not having much of a memory. It took a couple of minutes, but I was lucky enough to be right. Having failed to find a way out, it decided to hide in the cupboard in the corner of the room next to the window. Once it had settled down, I started to move slowly, approaching as quietly as I could with every effort turned to masking my psychic signature. With each pace I watched carefully for any sign that it had noticed me: one pace, no sign. The next pace, slow and steady – closing the distance. The third brought me next to the cupboard, looking down onto the spot where it was sitting obliviously, apparently ready for a nap. One deep breath. Another, preparing to act. As I started the third exhalation I reached out quickly and grabbed the thing, crushing it in my hands before it had time to react and immediately letting all the energy I'd stored in the waiting phase burst into the room to shake anything loose that we might have missed.

Nothing.

I called Nick in to check my findings and when he was happy we got Niki back in. She was better now, which made me much happier about things. We'd finished the top half of the building. We sent the others downstairs to get a drink while we got on with the bottom half. Frankly, they looked as though they needed it.

The next area for our attention was the bar. Now, if the place had been closed it wouldn't have been a problem, but The Griffin opened all day and by this point of the afternoon had a bar full of customers. Something a little more discreet was going to be required if we were to do the job without calling too much attention to ourselves. Nick and I discussed the situation, then he suggested a trawl. It was brilliant and, if it worked, nobody would suspect a thing. We set up shop in the back of the ground floor, behind the door that led from the private to the public part of the pub and then into the small backyard. First, we checked the area and found only a couple of minor things that were easily removed. Obviously, things were really only happening inside the building proper. With that done, I had my working area ready. Nick threw on his coat and left the yard through the gate directly out into the street and I settled in to wait.

While I was waiting, Nick was walking around the outside of the building to the front door and making himself the psychic equivalent of flypaper. The plan was for him to walk through the bar, catching everything within reach and dragging it all out to me where I had the equivalent of a psychic net ready to take his catch and secure it for us both to eliminate. This was one part of the plan that worked first time. Out came Nick, crawling with so many different things that I couldn't make out much detail and I ensnared the lot with one sweep and had wiped them out before it occurred to me that I was supposed to be waiting for Nick to help. That's reflex for you, I guess. I didn't want any of the catch to realise what was going on and start trying to fight back.

Nick stowed his coat upstairs and we walked into the bar, carefully scanning for anything that might have escaped his trawl. I took advantage of this to check the gents, since we had been going for a while and my ma always advised never to miss a chance at a rest break when the opportunity presents itself. I noticed that the chap Tim had identified as a 'gatekeeper' was sitting in his usual place and, judging from the look he gave me, he was not a member of the David Devereux Fan Club. I joined Nick at the table where the others were and explained what had happened. All we had left to do was the cellar.

Niki had told us that she particularly hated the cellar, which became obvious from her body language as she led us to the door. It stood next to the fireplace and as she unlocked the door we had a good chance to take a look at what Tim had called a 'gateway'. He was right, there was certainly some kind of link through to elsewhere and I was fairly sure that 'elsewhere' wasn't going to be a happy place full of rainbows and bunnies. But that was for later. Niki opened the cellar door for us and quickly stepped back to let us through.

I led the way and Nick came behind, throwing a shield between the cellar and the pub proper to make sure nothing tried getting away into a cleared area. The stairs were narrow, steep and just a little slippery and the atmosphere was more oppressive than anywhere else in the building and much colder than it had any right to be.

We started by looking for any point where ventilation opened to the outside and shielding it. Next was the delivery hatch that ran out onto the street, hidden behind a curtain. I had a very nasty feeling coming from there, so started by hitting it hard before I even looked through to see what was happening in there. I sealed the hatchway off at the doors, sterilised the barrel ramp with energy and then ran a shield over the curtain. Much better.

Nick, meanwhile, had been checking the area where barrels were stored and had a few spots he wanted my opinion on. My opinion by this point was, 'If it's not waving a white flag, blow it away!' and I demonstrated this with a casual brutality that surprised even me afterwards. Then I was on to the spirit store and I wasn't surprised to find more in there than just liquor. By this point the opposition was hardly even putting up a fight or attempting to get away and what we were finding was distinctly weaker. I took this as another good sign: if this was all that was left to fight back then we were nearly finished. Or more accurately, they were nearly finished.

It was almost no effort at all to eliminate what was left in the cellar by this point and frankly it was starting to feel more like a mercy killing with each one I destroyed. By the time I'd finished the joy of the hunt had finally passed and I was feeling rather sorry for the last few.

Nick, on the other hand, was very unhappy. He'd been doing the witch thing – talking to the wood of the building to get a measure of its condition and the state of the building in general. Whatever had been at work here had affected the wood like dry rot or woodworm, he told me, twisted it in such a way as to make it feel halfway between dead and wishing it was. With a clear working area, this was a job for him. I stood back and let him work, whispering under his breath and pushing energy into the beams, reminding them of spring, regeneration and good health. Once he'd finished, I prepared a burst of energy to detonate after we'd gone upstairs and Nick cleared out just ahead of me, feeling the warmth as the burst went off seconds after we'd closed the door.

Back to the others, to let them know that we were finally done. It was around five by this point, I think – we'd been hard at work for some time and both Nick and I were pretty tired. We headed upstairs to finish off the final details, with promises of beer to come once we'd done.

Back up in the kitchen, Nick and I considered the options for locking the place off to prevent anything recurring. We decided that the standard Athanor 'purge and shield' method would probably be best and set about getting ready for that. I also made a rare dip into ritual to construct a trap for anything that tried moving in to the cupboard where spider-mommy had been, with Nick's holy water and my rum glass. Since we'd worked the site together it seemed fitting to have a backup constructed from an element of each.

Consulting with Ian by phone, he agreed that, once we'd

closed down the gateway in the fireplace by the bar, he was happy to purge the building while Nick and I took care of the shielding. I mentioned the gateway to Nick and did a short exercise to disconnect it from anywhere it might have led. That finished, I looked across to Nick and told him what I'd done.

'Oh right,' he said, 'I've just dropped a ton of bricks on it as well!'

Between the two of us, though, we'd taken the gate out of operation. Ian hit the whole building with a blast of energy that set my teeth on edge and the two of us in the kitchen built a shield to seal the pub off from anything that might have been passing and thought the now-psychically-vacant pub might make a nice residence.

Job done.

We broke down our respective kit and put it away, collapsing the work area shielding from the kitchen to let it blend back into the rest of the pub now that it was safe to do so. As Nick was giving his final ritual thanks, I got a sense of something entirely different from a cupboard just into the corridor from the kitchen door. Letting Nick know what I was investigating, I opened the door for a look...

... and found something wonderful. Most old buildings have what is commonly referred to as a *genius loci*, a 'spirit of the place'. It's basically the building's sense of self, of place or of function, and pubs normally have quite a strong one because of the amount of sheer *living* that takes place in them. Here in this small cupboard we found what was left of The Griffin's. It's an odd experience even for me to step into a cupboard and feel suddenly more welcome than in any other place in a house, but that's exactly what happened here. I called Nick over and the grin on his face was a match to my own. We did what we could to feed it a little energy, to help it start to grow again. The most important thing, though, was that now the enormous amount of unpleasantness had been removed, it had a safe environment to grow back into. For me, that was one of the high points of the day.

Once we'd packed everything away, we went downstairs into the bar to witness my other high point: a table full of laughter. Niki was looking like an almost entirely different person and Baz and Jaine were far more relaxed, although Tim was looking sad. He explained that as we'd been finishing up he'd had one last message and, since he'd had the presence of mind to write it down on a beer mat, he showed it to me. The gist seemed to be 'We are leaving, goodbye.'

I explained to him that this was a good sign, not only because of the obvious change in Niki but also because whatever was causing the unpleasantness had finally gone. He agreed that the pub felt better, but felt sad for a while.

At Niki's insistence, the party began. There was beer and then Niki asserted that she made the world's finest Long Island Iced Tea and was ready to prove it to the Big City Boys. She was right. I'm not the world's biggest fan of the Iced Tea, but this was a doozy and several were consumed. We made arrangements to stay in the pub overnight, both to keep an eye on the place and allow Nick to have a few drinks to celebrate and unwind.

But Tim was still sad, even as the rest of the table celebrated. Niki and Jaine both tried to cheer him up a little but to no avail, so I took him for a walk around the graveyard opposite. This was his first serious encounter with the paranormal and it seemed that he had something of a sensitivity, so I explained a few of the basic facts of the life to him – things I've already told you in previous chapters – and recommended that he learn to develop personal shields to keep himself safe before anything unfortunate happened. He seemed better for it and it reminded me to recommend a couple of books on self-defence to all the people involved. I've mentioned them in the bibliography at the end of this book.

With Tim feeling better, we went back inside. The barrel was very firmly rolled out and a very happy atmosphere ruled the roost. Eventually, Tim, Jaine, Baz and Niki went off to a party and Nick and I joined a member of the bar staff to continue our own entertainments. There was a brief tour of some of Monmouth's other establishments and other people joined us later in the evening. There was singing, there were jokes, and a damned fine evening was had.

When I was discussing the case with Nick recently, as preparation for writing this chapter, he felt it was important to explain how much we drank as a good indicator of just how hard we'd worked and how much it took for us to relax after the job. Our best estimates are approximately 12 pints of beer and four or five Long Island Iced Teas each, followed by just under a bottle of whisky between the two of us, over a period of about ten hours, most of it in the first six. We felt we'd done a pretty heroic job and ended up doing some pretty heroic drinking.

Eventually, Nick went to bed in a fit of good sense, to be in a reasonable condition for travelling back the next day. I remained chatting with the two members of staff who lived on the premises in the front room. Unsurprisingly we discussed what had happened earlier in the day, especially how Niki had changed during the course of the day. While one of the staff didn't believe that paranormal phenomena exist, she did at least agree that Niki was looking better and we agreed to disagree about our views of the worlds in the interests of conviviality.

When dawn broke and the sound of birds waking up could be heard in the distance I'd pretty much reached the point where I was going to stay up all night and go to bed early the next day. But something was starting to niggle in the back of my head. Before I could put my finger on what was wrong, Nick burst into the room.

'Knife!' he said, looking straight at me. I stopped thinking and snapped straight back into sobriety.

'My kit bag. Kitchen. Black-handled dirk. Go!' Nick immediately shot off in search of my bag.

By the time I was on my feet and in pursuit, Nick was already on the upper floor at the top of the stairs. I could already feel something going wrong, the atmosphere of the place was starting to fog with an echo of what we'd removed. I heard a thump, and some swearing, then Nick came back with a bleeding hand muttering unkind things about my kit. I dressed the wound as he explained what he'd just done. The atmosphere was clearing again but I wanted to know what it was he'd picked up and what he'd done about it.

He had woken suddenly just as the sun came over the horizon and had sensed the same thing I had. He'd recognised that whatever had caused the difficulties was leaking back through the shields and from his bed in the en suite room he'd realised where the leak was entering the building, the same cupboard where spider-mommy had given us all the trouble earlier. Nick had earthed the energy coming through by planting my dirk in the floor of the cupboard and sliced his hand a little as it slid down from the handle. It seemed reasonable, in magic a little blood can go a long way. Whatever it was that we were dealing with, we'd knocked it on the head for the day.

I took a look at the shields and realised why they'd sprung a leak. There was a wave of aggression, fear and all sorts of other nasty stuff piled up against the shields to such an extent that I was amazed they hadn't crashed entirely. Something was quite spectacularly wrong and I wanted to know what it was. But first things first. I diverted the pile of energy sitting on our shield toward the river, so that it would be washed away and disposed of as safely as possible. Then I reinforced the shield to repair the damage it had taken. I didn't want to be caught napping if a second wave hit us. Then I sent Nick back to bed and started to look at what had happened.

The first, and most obvious, detail was that this wasn't natural. A scan of the surrounding area indicated that it had just been effectively sucked clean of its negative energy to make that wave. Widening the scan further showed that the entire town was the same. This was someone's doing, a deliberate act, but why hadn't they followed through? Surely if they'd got us to a point where the shields were giving way then they'd want to hit us again and breach the shields? There was more to this than met the eye.

Up to this point, I'd thought that previous attempts to sort the problem hadn't worked because nobody had been up into the loft to take out the brain. With the new information, however, this was obviously wrong. Someone wanted The Griffin the way it was, and I wanted to know who and why.

It seemed to me that either the magician responsible (and it had to be a magician since no natural thing could have pulled that trick on us) had used everything they had to pile that mountain of energy on us and was lying doggo to see what we'd do next or there was no specific control over what had just happened. I sat quietly in the front room and started to breathe, centring myself for a scan of the surrounding area to hunt for any signs of magical activity. I was alone, since somewhere in the fuss my two companions had decided to go to bed.

I opened my awareness out, letting it flow over the town to see if I could spot any activity. It took a while, because it was a fairly large area to cover, but I didn't find anything specific. There were certainly groups working in the town, but no sign of anyone just having done anything like what we'd just experienced. I was tired, sure, and dealing with the beginnings of a hangover, but I felt pretty confident that I'd still be able to spot something that big. That left me, though, with the rather odd conclusion that this was a regular thing, an automatic process.

But why? Why would somebody want to drop all the crud in an area on one spot like this on a regular basis? Nick got to the answer just before me: the gateway.

Someone had come up with the ingenious idea of pulling as much negative energy as they could out of the town and flushing it through the gateway in the pub fireplace. It couldn't come in at ground level or anyone walking the streets would be hit with it, so it would need a high access point like the spider-mommy cupboard, which was only about eight feet from the fireplace in the horizontal plane. It explained why the pub was so seriously screwed up as well: with that happening on a regular basis all sorts of nasty side-effects were going to crop up and it would certainly explain why Niki was unable to sleep in the place. If she was picking even a fragment of this up then her nights would not be peaceful.

Feeling pretty good about this as a theory, I decided to get sleep. I woke up a couple of hours later without the hangover that had been creeping up previously. Once Nick was up and had consumed a litre or two of coffee, we struck out for breakfast and discussed our options. What it came down to was that someone had done this deliberately and would undoubtedly be planning to put things back the way they were. What we needed was a plan to stop anyone else from getting hurt because of it.

As we brought the car back to the pub from the place we'd parked on the other side of town, the plan came into focus. We'd need help, but I knew who to call. I set up an appointment with the relevant person for later that same day, so we'd have things in place and ready to go by the next sunrise. Everything that could be done, had been done.

We had breakfast in the pub, collected our kit together and loaded it into the car, then we said our goodbyes and left the pub for the last time. As we did, we met Niki and Baz coming in from their party. They both looked happy – much more so than they had at the same time the previous day. I was glad to have a chance to say goodbye and so were they. Then Nick and I got into the car, wound down the windows, turned up the stereo and headed for home. As we crossed the town boundary, I looked at my watch. We'd been in Monmouth for twenty-four hours, almost to the minute.

There are some details I've deliberately missed out of the story. I have, for example, a pretty good idea of at least the type of group responsible for what we found, and strong suspicions of its exact identity. I've omitted those suspicions because I can't afford a libel case and because I know that they have better lawyers than I do. I wouldn't be surprised if they were still trying to put things back the way they were, too. Hopefully, that won't be happening in a hurry.

I did indeed brief the person I'd arranged to see and they made arrangements to have the energy diverted on a more permanent basis than I'd been able to sort on the fly. To my knowledge those arrangements are still in place.

I also heard from Niki a couple of months back. She'd been getting a few problems with seeing some of the figures from the pub in other places. I recommended a course of action and asked her to get in touch if it didn't work. She had a medium to work with there and I spent some time running through things with her, making sure that she was happy to take care of things and that she'd also get in touch if things went awry. Since I've not heard back from either of them, I'm hoping that all is well there now. She had left The Griffin shortly after Nick and I had been there, as she had already planned. After everything that had happened to her, I can't blame her in the least.

chapter thirteen
FAST AND DIRTY

'No battle plan ever survives first contact with the enemy'
Napoleon Bonaparte

Up until now, I've been waxing lyrical about the benefits of research and how it's absolutely essential to getting the job done properly. Now don't get me wrong, it is. But there are occasions when you just don't have the time. This is where all the training, all the study and a whole pile of luck come together, because you end up in a fight against opponents about whom you have no idea. The trouble is that, if you try to play things fast and loose, it's even riskier than taking on something you *know* you can't handle. This is why I say it's stupid to go in and do this on your own, with no backup, no research and no equipment.

This is the story of a night when I was stupid, and really, really lucky.

This was back in the early days of Athanor. Work was slow, so I was working behind the bar of a pub in Bristol. It was a job I thoroughly enjoyed, since I'm very fond of beer and was learning a great deal about it by virtue of having one of the best cellar men in town teaching me. It wasn't a secret in the pub that I was doubling up with Athanor, although most people didn't want to know particularly about it. It was more a matter of 'Oh that's Doc, he's an exorcist when he's not pouring beer' than any kind of great excitement, and that was very much the way I liked it.

A PhD student at the university, Pete, was one of our regulars. He only lived around the corner and, since he was fond of a decent pint, we were his local. He was a good chap – intelligent, personable – extremely good company, and we became friends. One night while we were out for a drink socially he said those famous words, 'We've got a ghost at our place, actually.'

Now those words can frequently cause my heart to sink. But Pete was a friend. We'd got on for a while, I knew his girlfriend, Kate. He raised the topic gently rather the more usual, 'Oh, he works with spooky things – let's talk of spooky things and be interesting!' which makes me want to run screaming without even stopping to finish my drink. So I probed a little, since I had the impression that he felt uncomfortable mentioning it to me.

It turned out that there was something in his bedroom. The tale he told was a familiar one, but that never makes it any better for the teller, or any easier – a strange feeling in the room, Kate having trouble sleeping there, weird dreams she couldn't quite remember but that left her feeling upset and poorly rested and feelings of general discomfort in there. It was making life uncomfortable, but not unbearable. Knowing he was trying to build up to asking me if I'd be willing to help, I decided to pre-empt him (and take some of the weight off his shoulders) by offering to take a look.

We then proceeded to get drunk and forget all about it, as Pete's relief was obvious. I could see how much effort it had taken him to ask – not only because he knew that under normal circumstances there was no way he could have afforded my professional fees, but also because he seemed to think he was imposing. He might have been a little, but friends are there to help where they can. I have a wide circle of acquaintance, but few close friends. The close friends are the ones you know would drop everything for you and that cuts both ways.

A few weeks later I was tending bar and Pete walked in. He'd been meaning to catch up with me because they were about to head off on holiday in the next few days and the flat was due to be fumigated to deal with an insect nest in the building while they were away. He thought he'd mention this since he'd heard me say that a thorough clean-out can be a good thing once an entity had been removed from a place, just to give the place some fresh air and remove any lingering traces after the clearout. It just helps things feel nice again.

I thought about my diary between then and his departure date. Then I heard myself say the fatal words: 'Well, I finish here at midnight. If I come over, will you be up?' Oddly enough, he was willing to wait up and have me come over. So bang went that get-out clause.

So midnight rolled round. I finished sending drunks home and helping clean the pub, dropped over to the corner shop for a packet of cigarettes and set out for Pete's place chanting psychic power-up mantras in my head as I went.

Pete and Kate lived in a reasonably sized ground-floor flat with two bedrooms, a kitchen, living room and bathroom. They'd been lucky enough to find a nice flat in a nice location, not even a great distance from town. It was neat and tidy, tastefully decorated, pretty much what you'd expect from any couple in their late twenties – apart from the vast pile of scientific papers and handwritten notes around the computer desk in the corner.

We started with a coffee, as the tale was told to me again. It was pretty much as I remembered and, with the upcoming clear-out and clean through, it struck me as ideal timing. At this point I was assuming it to be a fairly standard psychic area effect such as a build-up of negative energy dispersing into the environment, since the effects sounded about right and such things are far more common in my experience than actual ghosts. I finished my cigarette and took a wander round the place. The living room was clear – I'd been sitting in it for a good quarter of an hour and there were no signs of anything I wouldn't expect to find in my own living room. Next was the kitchen – clear again. Likewise the bathroom and the second bedroom. So the only place left to check was the main bedroom, which was the only place Pete had reported as having any activity.

From the moment I crossed the threshold of that bedroom I could feel a distinct presence. Probing a little further, I was able to determine that it certainly seemed to be the ghost of an actual dead person as opposed to any of the more common alternatives. The dead feel different from most of what I see – there's more of a sense of a real personality than with astral entities, thought-forms or demonic activity. Less of a sense of wrongness, but still a feeling of something out of place. There's no real hard and fast rule, but the difference is there and, if you're capable of picking anything like this up at all, you can usually spot it. Carefully ensuring that the room was sealed with a temporary psychic shield, I withdrew to the living room to make my report. My news was received as ever with a great sigh of relief. It's reassuring to have somebody come and tell you that you're not mad and even more so when that person then tells you that it's a fixable situation.

So there I was, sitting in a flat in the centre of Bristol with no backup, no kit, no real plan, sod all background research and a dead man down the corridor who needs to be evicted.

'Oh bugger,' I said to myself. 'Still, best be getting on with it!'

These are the times when all the training, all the work, all the background comes into play. When you're effectively stuck in the woods and have to improvise. I knew my friends were counting on me and there was no time for me to come back and look at it once I'd tooled up. So I had to improvise.

First up – the contents of my pockets. OK, I had a lighter. Good start. Fire's never a bad thing to have knocking about the place (as long as it's under control) under these circumstances. Nothing else of any real use, though. Time for another cigarette while I thought about it.

One cigarette later inspiration struck and it was time for action. Surprising as it may sound, the contents of an average kitchen can supply everything you need to perform an exorcism – if you know what you're doing. So I started wandering through the cupboards, watched by two very bemused-looking people. I knew what I needed; it was just a matter of making it. I sent Kate off to get me a bottle of perfume with an atomiser top – incense substitute. Knowing she took her faith seriously, I also asked for a Bible. That was going to come in handy another way, but I'll explain that when it comes up. Since I'd managed to get myself ordained a couple of years previously (don't ask) Holy Water wasn't a problem either. Scented tea lights double up as ritual candles and a freshly sharpened pencil would do as a substitute magic wand at a pinch.

I looked at my improvised gear and assessed my chances of getting away with it. With a silent prayer to anyone who might have been paying attention, I threw a cup of coffee down my neck to help get my blood pressure and sugar levels up a bit and started setting my gear up in the bedroom.

It was Showtime. I walked into the room, and closed the door behind me, giving strict instructions that I was not to be disturbed before dawn.

The moment I closed the door, the atmosphere changed

and the temperature dropped a little. It knew I was there and it was quite obviously less than impressed by the fact. I could feel it watching me as I started to set up my kit and place a candle at each of what I guessed to be the cardinal points of the compass, the traditional places to mark when starting most kinds of magic. With those lit, I went through the rest of a brief but effective ritual to set up a circle of protection – a safe working area – in much the same way that I would at the beginning of a more formal working. This was as big as I could make it, covering the centre of the room and as much of the rest of it as possible. There was no way to include the wardrobe or the other corners of the room, but it was enough to hold the ghost captive. Secure that the circle would contain what was to follow, I sat down on the bed for a moment, wanting to get a sense of the room. It wasn't a large room – big enough for two people but hardly what I'd call luxurious. There was a wardrobe in one corner, a double bed in the middle of a wall and a table by the window. There was a small cabinet on each side of the bed and the one nearest the door now held my improvised gear, laid out ready for use. I had placed lit candles on the table by the window, on a patch of floor by the wardrobe and on the two bedside cabinets. The door was in the corner behind me, opposite the window and facing the wardrobe to my right.

The ghost was trying to throw my concentration, making unexpected noises in random parts of the space and trying unsuccessfully to knock things over. Various knick-knacks and Kate's lotions and potions on the window table started wobbling. The candle furthest from me by the window suddenly went out. I calmly walked across the room and relit it. Another, back by the door where I'd been sitting. I did likewise. While it was trying to unsettle me, I was getting its measure. Although I'd been apparently confident in front of my friends, I had been nervous about all the things that could go wrong – not being able to set things up the way I'd normally want to, the possibility of it being just too much for me to handle solo, potential injury from poltergeist activity… A list of possible bad outcomes that was far longer than the good. But there was no time for that now. I'd started and had to see it through. I'd worry about the casualty lists caused by hubris and making all those promises about not being so damned cocky next time if I got out of there.

I smiled to myself, 'I've got the kit, I've got the skills, and I've got your number, sunshine. Let's dance.'

Having worked out the best spot in the room through a combination of training and guesswork, I performed a ritual to open what's best described as a doorway to the lands of the Dead just inside the circle by the candle in the window. This isn't so much a physical thing, but performs the same function in these circumstances. I needed a focal point for him to make the transition from Here to There and, since he wasn't going to be staying Here, that's where he was going, whether he liked it or not. By this point I'd definitely got the impression that our target was male – I'm still not exactly sure why, but I knew it had to be a man. Since the doorway held, I must have guessed the right spot close enough for my purposes. I locked it down for the moment, but had it ready to open with as little effort on my part as possible. If I had to rough-house this one out, I didn't want to be wasting time on rituals I could set up in advance. Of course, at the same time I didn't want anything else trying to come through the other way so that's why I locked it.

The target was not at all happy to see that door go up. Candles started going out again, but I just kept relighting them. There was a sound that might have been moaning. I figured that if he wanted to expend energy like that I was happy to let him, much like playing a fish on the hook before you reel them in. Finally, I decided it was time to start phase two and get his attention.

The perfume atomiser was, as I said, to be my incense substitute. Using my lighter as the ignition I started by perfuming the quarters as marked by the candles and then started to circle the room clockwise. With each step I gave another puff from the atomiser, which the lighter turned into a small orange fireball. I could feel the air was thicker in front of me, so I was driving the target ahead and, by the time I'd finished circling the room (including a not particularly dignified part where I had to crawl over the bed), the only way out for this fellow was the doorway I'd set up, inside the circle.

Next up, the improvised Holy Water. Now this isn't a normal part of my kit, but I was working without a metaphorical safety net and figured therefore that I needed all the help I could get. A sprinkling around the floor and across all the surfaces and objects within the circle meant that he wasn't going to be able to start throwing stuff at me. Given that I had no sense of foreign-ness or exotic auras I guessed he was most likely to have been a Christian in life, so a drop of the good stuff would most likely stop him from trying anything too clever. Under most circumstances this would have been a dangerous supposition to make, as in my experience Christian imagery isn't necessarily the best thing to use against non-Christian things, but it seemed right to me and I've always been a big fan of my hunches.

With that done, I was feeling a lot better about my situation. This guy may well have had the ability to affect flames and such, but his best distraction attempts thus far had yielded no results. While he'd been making his presence felt by creating spots and extinguishing candles, I'd calmly, deliberately and methodically marked his territory as my own. I'd changed the rules of his game under him. It was no longer a case of the living invading his space: he was very much in mine.

Time for phase three.

'Right, sunshine. Listen in.' It was a solid voice, with a pile of Chi-loaded subsonic resonance on the side for good measure. I've noticed that, while you might get a response from a conversational tone, loading some power behind your voice really does make a difference. It was a trick I learned in my first séance when I was seventeen. 'You're leaving. You're not welcome here and you're making the people who should be here uncomfortable. It's time to go.'

Well, there's nothing like a good solid statement of intent and that one just placed my balls quite comprehensively in the sling. Even if I'd had a chance to balk before then, there was no way I was getting out of that room until the job was done. Not that I had any intention of making a run for it. I was starting to feel much more confident about this whole thing working and knew full well he'd be ten times harder to shift if I had to make a second attempt. So I was in for the duration – death or glory style. No problem. Well, not much problem.

He'd been trying to spread himself out across the circle rather than coalescing into one place, probably trying to make it difficult for me to get a decent lock on him. It was a reasonable response, but he'd left it too late for that and was starting to realise his mistake. Complacency can cause all kinds of mistakes and, while I'd been very carefully avoiding it, it seemed that he hadn't. It struck me that he was used to ordinary people without any training and he'd probably never come across someone like me before.

Realising that diffusing was getting him nowhere and that there weren't any cracks in the circle for him to exploit, he started to coalesce. This was my best sense yet of what I was actually dealing with – up to now I'd been running on solid basic principles and a fair chunk of luck. What we had seemed to be a man in his mid-forties, not too bright and not too happy about having me speak to him in a less than friendly way. He locked eyes with me and started to attempt to drain some of my energy to buoy him up for the inevitable fight that was fast approaching. I smiled, 'Nice try, matey, but no cigar.'

The word 'cigar' seemed to trigger a memory for him. I got a sense of the dockyards, the smell of tobacco smoke, thoughts of beer. I felt he might have worked nearby because Bristol has a history not only as a port but also as a centre of the tobacco industry in the UK. I couldn't be sure and couldn't tie it to anything, as I'd not researched the location and what might have been there before. It certainly seemed that the building had gone up around him rather than vice versa. Of course, none of this was relevant. He was moving on whether he wanted to or not.

Breaking his attempted connection, I pulled a fast one and slammed a connection of my own onto him, one designed to lock him into his current form for ease of handling while making sure his energy levels were held firmly in check – think of it as a psychic arm lock. He made a break for the wardrobe, but the circle stopped him before he could get there and I was able to get hold of him for the first time as I felt my hand close on a shoulder made of thickened air. At last, he understood what had happened. He was trapped with something he couldn't handle, couldn't control. The environment he had controlled had been taken away from him and there was nothing he could do about it. His reaction was the same that you'd expect from a living person under such circumstances – he panicked. He started expending energy left, right and centre, flailing around and at me in an attempt to break my concentration. I could feel slight brushes of contact where his fists were attempting to flail at my body and hitting the protections I normally use to keep myself safe. If I let this carry on there'd be no telling what might happen – he might even expend so much of his energy that there wouldn't be enough of him to get a decent grip on. So it was time to try a slightly desperate gambit. I reached out, closed my hand in the appropriate area, spun his shoulder round, looked him square in the area of thickened air that passed for his face and pointed out one small detail he might have missed.

'For crying out loud, mate, you're bloody dead!'

And it worked. The news hit him like a cricket bat. The entire performance – all the thrashing, all the panic, all the anger – just stopped. I could feel him there, like a man in shock, working out the truth of what I'd told him. I smiled sadly at him, 'Sorry, mate, that's just the way it is. Nothing personal.'

After that, it was easy to get him to make the crossover. When it gets to this stage it's very much like walking a drunk out of a pub at the end of the night – 'You've had enough, time to go home'. I opened the gate that I'd set up earlier and, one arm around his shoulders, walked him to it. I could feel him crying, a distinct sense of sobbing – what of his friends? His family? I couldn't tell him. Odds are they'd be waiting for him when he got wherever he was going. We got to the gate, I patted him on the back and he stepped through.

Clearing up was a fairly swift process. Permanently close and remove the doorway – very carefully. Blow out the candles, turn on the lights and open a window to clear the slightly odd smell. Then open the door and report back. Apparently about two and a half hours had passed.

While I grabbed a large scotch and lit a cigarette, Pete and

Kate went to inspect my handiwork. Their reaction is one you get used to pretty quickly – amazement at the difference, a lightening of the heart and an outpouring of relief mixed with happiness. That doesn't mean it gets old or that you don't enjoy it every time. We sat and chatted for a while, until the adrenaline started wearing off and I remembered it was about four in the morning and I'd been on my feet for sixteen hours.

As the sky started to lighten in the east, I wandered back into the city centre smoking my last cigarette. I hopped into a cab, got home and slept the sleep of the incredibly lucky.

Oh yes, the Bible. That was a McGuffin. I knew that Kate took her faith very seriously indeed, so I took it in with me to give her more confidence in what I was about to do. Much like the Holy Water, in fact. The thing about magic is that it seems to work better (in my understanding) if you've got a load of people who believe it will. It's like the big rituals with robes and props and everything else – they're there to help you believe that what you're going to do will work. Take all that positive thinking stuff and run with it – it's no different. We control our own reality through what we believe to be true. Because what I had to work with was a fairly solid Roman Catholic, I went for some extra Christian imagery to boost her faith. With that and the fact that I expected the ghost to be fairly Christian, it couldn't exactly hurt.

As I said, that one was fast, dirty and ran on luck and cigarette smoke.

AFTERWORD

So there we are. If I've managed to get this right, I've hopefully given you a glimpse behind the curtain to see what happens in a world you'll probably never have to visit. It's different, sure, but it's out there and it's just as real as anything else you deal with. Just remember that I've picked out the interesting bits where I can and that most of the time situations like this can be dealt with a lot more smoothly. The trouble is that smooth is boring, so don't think I'm a screw-up because I've shown two decades worth of 'not quite according to plan' in one book.

If you are experiencing a difficulty of this nature, please don't contact me directly. I'm part of a company that I won't pimp here, but it can be found easily enough and there are others out there who provide the same service. The trick is not to panic, but to get someone in who can help.

Thanks for your company along the way. I hope you enjoyed it.

GLOSSARY

Artificial Elemental
See Tulpa.

Astral travel
The process of sending one's mind elsewhere for whatever purpose, while the body remains in position. Out-of-body experiences are a limited form of this.

Chaos Magic
Coined originally by Peter Carroll in his book *Liber Null*, but rooted in the earlier work of Austin Osman Spare and Aleister Crowley, Chaos Magic is based upon the freedom to shift between paradigms as required. For example, to perform a ritual from the Golden Dawn system, followed by a banishing that uses a Chinese rite. The important factor is that the practitioner is able to focus absolute belief in the task at hand. The term has been misused widely in popular culture, generally by using the name (because it sounds cool) but none of the actual techniques.

Dee, John (1527–1608 or 1609)
British mathematician, alchemist, occultist, astronomer, astrologer and geographer who acted as a consultant to Queen Elizabeth I. He is also believed to have played a role in the development of cryptography and to have worked for

Sir Francis Walsingham as an intelligence agent, possibly the first British spy to hold the number '007'. He suggested the idea of a national library, which was sadly rejected, and his private library was widely thought to be one of the finest in Europe. He was also an early proponent of British colonisation of the Americas and the idea of a British Empire that spanned the world.

His most famous magical work was undertaken with the medium Edward Kelley, and involved contacting a number of what he believed were Angels, who laid down an entire system of language that is now known as Enochian (*see below*), and dictated several books to him. Dee's notes from these communications were collected by Henry Casaubon in the book *A True & Faithful Relation of What passed for many Yeers between Dr. John Dee (A Mathematician of Great Fame in Q. Eliz. and King James their Reignes) and some spirits* in 1659.

Enochian

Supposedly the language of the angels as related to John Dee (*see above*) and Edward Kelley, although other versions exist from other people, it is now considered by most magical practitioners more likely to be a constructed language. It is used in a number of schools of magic, most notably Thelema, the Golden Dawn system and LaVeyan Satanism.

There is also a class of magic known by the same name, which relates to dealing with angels.

The word 'Enochian' refers to the *Book of Enoch*, a pseudepigraphal text and a major source for the study of Judeo-Christian angels. It relates the life of the prophet Enoch, the great-grandfather of Noah, and describes how the angels who fell from Heaven asked him to intercede with God on their behalf, Enoch's visionary journey to Heaven and the revelations he received while there.

Genius Loci

In modern usage, *genius loci* normally refers to a location's distinctive atmosphere, or a 'spirit of place'. The term is originally found in Roman mythology, where it referred to the protective spirit of a place and was often depicted as a snake.

Great Cthulhu

Invented by the 1920s author Howard Philips Lovecraft, Cthulhu is a member of the race known as the Great Old Ones. It and its fellows ruled over the Earth long before the coming of man and Cthulhu is said to lie dormant in the city of R'Lyeh, deep beneath the Pacific Ocean. Cthuloid magic is popular in some quarters, particularly with chaos magicians, but it's not a style I personally favour.

Hermetic Order of the Golden Dawn

Formed originally in 1888, and known more generally as the 'Golden Dawn', this organisation is probably the single greatest influence on twentieth century western occultism. Concepts of spirituality, magic and ritual that became core elements of many other traditions, including Wicca, Thelema and other forms of magical spirituality popular today, are drawn from the Golden Dawn traditions. Notable members of the organisation include A. E. Waite (of Rider-Waite Tarot fame), W. B. Yeats, S. L. Macgregor Mathers and Aleister Crowley.

The term 'Hermetic' relates to the precepts of occult philosophy laid down by Hermes Trimegistus (Thrice-Great Hermes), identified as an ancient Egyptian scholar and priest, who is considered synonymous with the Egyptian god Thoth.

Libation

A liquid offering, primarily for religious purposes.

Long Island Iced Tea
A cocktail, the origins of which are hotly debated in some quarters. One popular version in the UK mixes equal parts vodka, gin, rum, tequila and triple sec with lemon juice and a splash of cola. Most places add far too much cola for my taste.

Obsidian
A volcanic glass used in ancient Central American ritual. The Toltecs used it to make knives and other objects of importance. When highly polished, it makes an effective mirror and an example of this can be seen in the British Museum in the collection of artefacts believed to have been owned by Dr John Dee, as he used a mirror believed to be of Aztec origin for scrying.

Phurba
From Tibetan shamanism (*see below*). A three-bladed knife with the head of a three-faced demon modelled at the hilt and an eagle's head holding the blades in its beak. The phurba is the traditional magical weapon of the shaman in Tibet, used for killing demons. I have one also and am very fond of it.

When used during exorcism, the phurba is used to hold demons in place once they have been removed from their places of hiding or human hosts. It can also be used to control negative energies from a person or group, allowing the wielder to deal with those energies as appropriate

Portal/Dimensional Gate
A term of convenience, used here to denote a point where the barrier between here and elsewhere is thin enough to penetrate. Examples are places like stone circles, although such places are not always marked in such a convenient fashion. Gates can also be opened temporarily with magic to either

summon something (a demon, to use an extreme example) or send something away as in chapter thirteen, where one is used as a point of transition for the entity's convenience.

RSPK (Recurrent Spontaneous PsychoKinetic phenomena)
More commonly known as 'poltergeist activity', this is a generic term for things moving without physical intercession. It covers everything from a glass wobbling on a shelf to furniture throwing itself across a room.

Scrying
The act of magically observing things from a distance. This differs from remote sensing because a device (such as a mirror or crystal ball) is used as a means to reveal the image rather than transport one's entire consciousness.

Sigil
A symbol created for a specific magical purpose. The term sigil comes from the Latin word *sigillum* meaning 'seal'. A sigil may have an abstract, pictorial or semi-abstract form, and can appear in any medium or as a visualisation in the mind of the magician. Visual symbols are the most popular form, but the use of sound or tactile symbols in magic is not unknown.

Smudge Stick
A Native American item. A bundle of herbs, based on White Sage, used in space-clearing techniques. They frequently smell awful.

Spirits, Elemental
A spirit comprised of, or strongly attuned with, one of the classical elements defined by Paracelsus in the sixteenth

century. They are mentioned in a wide range of magical books and can be summoned magically, but are generally happy to go about their own business unless interfered with.

In modern magic the word Elemental can also be used to describe what I have referred to here as a Tulpa.

Tantra
A group of esoteric traditions from the Indian subcontinent and Asia. A form of Tantra exists in the Buddhist, Hindu and Bönpo faiths and can be dated back to the middle of the first millennium. It experienced a surge of popularity during the 1960s as part of the New Age movement.

Technomancy
A magical approach that blends ancient and modern, approaching magic as though it worked on the same lines as electronic equipment. This term also includes the magical charging and modification of modern devices to assist the magician and is as good a way as I can think of to stop Windows crashing when I'm halfway through a paragraph.

Thought Form
See Tulpa.

Tibetan Shamanism
The traditional pre-Buddhist beliefs of Tibet, also practised in Nepal and Bhutan. One of the primary duties of a shaman in Tibet is to deal with demons and as a result they have developed some of the most effective techniques I know to do just that.

For more information, I recommend reading Alexandra David-Néel's excellent book *Magic and Mystery in Tibet.*

Tulpa/Thought Form/Artificial Elemental

An entity created from psychic energy, either to perform a specific purpose or spontaneously from a mixture of ambient energy and powerful emotion. See chapter four for more information.

When specifically called into being by a magician, they are generally referred to as Servitors. References to this kind of tulpa can be found in the works of Austin Osman Spare and Aleister Crowley. They are a frequently used device in modern Chaos Magic.

Vodoun (also spelled Voodoo, Vodou, Vudu)

A religion practised in the Caribbean, South America, West Africa and famously in Louisiana, USA. It is far too complex and subtle a subject to cover here, and there is a great deal of literature available on the subject.

Water Spirit / Undine

See Spirits, Elemental.

FURTHER READING

As I'm sure you can imagine, I've read a lot of books on this sort of thing over the years. Below I present a small list of books that I would recommend if you wish to take an interest in the subjects I've covered any further.

Psychic Self-Defence – Dion Fortune (1930)
Written over seventy-five years ago and still a classic text, this book draws heavily on Fortune's own experiences. I feel that it's important to take her attitudes with a pinch of salt, as they are very much of her time. Her opinions of the 'Witch Cult', for example, and her antipathy towards the work of Aleister Crowley are not necessarily ones with which I would agree, but if the reader is able to stay with her then this book has a lot to recommend it. It's well written and Fortune knows when to inject a little wit to keep things flowing.

The book contains a great deal of good, sensible advice about what to do if one believes oneself to be the victim of a psychic attack, starting with the admonishment not to jump to conclusions and following through with practical steps that can be taken to deal with the problem in a fashion I feel is more solidly effective than some modern texts on the subject. One point on which it could be said to fall down is in the area between psychic attack and mental illness, but then a great deal has been learned since the book was written.

This was the first book on the occult that I read, and one

I continue to recommend to clients who need to ensure continuing protection after we have finished assisting them.

Barefoot Doctor's Handbook for the Urban Warrior – Stephen Russell (1998)
Quite simply, this is my favourite book about energy work. Russell (or 'Barefoot Doctor' as he's generally known) is a healer trained in Chinese medicine and psychotherapy, and teaches tai chi, meditation and the philosophy and techniques of Taoism, and I can also tell you from experience that he's a terribly nice fellow. His style is light-hearted and easy to read, but this doesn't mean that he misses out anything important. His techniques (for this is very much a practical book) are likewise delivered with a sense of humour but are most certainly effective and cover everything from basic shielding, to enhancing energy flow, learning to meditate and even a little wardrobe advice. I've given more copies of this book away than I like to think about, and normally replace them pretty quickly.

You don't even need to buy into the philosophy if you don't want to: the exercises work either way.

Condensed Chaos – Phil Hine (1995)
Probably the best book on magic I've ever read. Phil Hine is one of the great figures of the Chaos Magic movement, and in this book he explains it clearly and sensibly. The ideas skip esoteric language wherever possible and are designed specifically to be workable. It also takes time out to explain the possible down-sides of practising magic, complete with tips on what to look for so remedial action can be taken sooner rather than later. Happily, this section comes before the practical bits, which contain few rituals but concentrates on giving information that the reader can work with.

This is a book filled with humour and common sense, that manages to avoid the dry, dusty approach or self-conscious esotericism all too common in books on the subject. While some people say that Hine's work is meant for the beginner, I disagree. It's certainly designed to be accessible, but I feel that he has a great deal to say to, and be learned by, magicians of all levels.

On-line resources

The two main references that I use are Wikipedia (http://www.wikipedia.org) and Thelemapedia (http://www.thelemapedia.org/index.html). Wikipedia is the justly-famous open-source encyclopaedia, and I find it an invaluable aid to research since it covers a wide range of esoteric subjects as well as the more mundane. Thelemapedia is organised along similar lines, but specialises in Thelema and magical theory.